STUDIES

OF

BLAST FURNACE PHENOMENA.

STUDIES

OF

BLAST FURNACE PHENOMENA.

BY

M. L. GRUNER,
PRESIDENT OF THE GENERAL COUNCIL OF MINES OF FRANCE,
AND LATELY PROFESSOR OF METALLURGY AT THE ÉCOLE DES MINES.

*TRANSLATED, WITH THE AUTHOR'S SANCTION,
WITH AN APPENDIX,*

BY L. D. B. GORDON, F.R.S.E., F.G.S.,
EMERITUS REGIUS PROFESSOR OF CIVIL ENGINEERING AND MECHANICS IN THE UNIVERSITY OF GLASGOW, FORMERLY A STUDENT OF THE ROYAL SCHOOL OF MINES, OF FREIBERG, IN SAXONY; HONORARY MEMBER OF THE INSTITUTION OF ENGINEERS AND SHIP-BUILDERS IN SCOTLAND; MEMBER OF THE IRON AND STEEL INSTITUTE.

PHILADELPHIA:
HENRY CAREY BAIRD,
INDUSTRIAL PUBLISHER,
406 WALNUT STREET.
1874.

PHILADELPHIA:
COLLINS, PRINTER,
705 Jayne Street.

CONTENTS.

SECTION VII.

SECTION VIII.

SECTION IX.

SECTION X.

SECTION XI.

SECTION XII.

SECTION XIII.

SECTION XIV.

SECTION XV.

SECTION XVI.

SECTION XVII.

SECTION XVIII.

SECTION XIX.

SECTION XX.

SECTION XXI.

SECTION XXII.

SECTION XXIII.

SECTION XXIV.

SECTION XXV.

SECTION XXVI.

SECTION XXVII.

SECTION XXVIII.

APPENDIX.

To ISAAC LOWTHIAN BELL, Esq.,

President of the Iron and Steel Institute.

My dear Bell,

In the hope of being useful to members of the Iron and Steel Institute, and others who do not read technical literature in foreign languages, this translation of M. Gruner's "Études sur les Hauts-Fourneaux" was undertaken. You have allowed me to dedicate the translation to you. No one having any knowledge of the subject will ask my reason for doing so.

M. Gruner has methodically digested and arranged several important sections of your experiments and observations, and has thus rendered the results you have published more readily available to many who desire to inform themselves of the progress made in the application of exact science to blast furnace practice, and who lack the habits of study necessary for the full appreciation of your original work.

The series of memoirs you have published in the Journal of the Iron and Steel Institute, on the chemical phenomena of iron-smelting—your careful diligence in the experimental verification of your observations in working furnaces, and your philosophical views in combining and reasoning upon them—have identified your name with the recent progress towards an exact theory of that wonderfully perfect apparatus, the Blast Furnace.

You for the first time connected the Chemical and

Calorific phenomena of the Blast Furnace together with such precision as permits us to calculate, with the certainty of a near approximation to the truth, the *technical* useful effect of any furnace, and the *economical* effect of furnaces working in any district for which the proportions of fuel, ores, and fluxes, and the temperature of the blast are known.

The results of your observations, and the numerous facts elicited from many practical men in the "discussions" at the meetings of the Iron and Steel Institute, are indeed the groundwork of M. Gruner's "Studies," in which he establishes Analytical Formulas by which all the necessary calculations can be readily worked.

The happy remembrances of thirty-three years' social intercourse and sympathy in the study of science applied to the arts, is an independent reason for my offering you this tribute of my friendship and esteem.

Believe me to be,

Yours sincerely,

LEWIS D. B. GORDON.

TOTTERIDGE, August, 1873.

TRANSLATOR'S PREFACE.

THE Studies of Blast Furnace Phenomena by M. Gruner are not written in a style that "those who run may read;" but whoever will take the pains to read them will find his reward in a more exact appreciation of how the recent investigations of Mr. Bell and others into the chemical and calorific phenomena of the blast furnace may be practically applied to questions of blast furnace economy.

For the last three years the question of the *minimum cost, theoretically and practically, of producing a ton of pig-iron* has chiefly occupied the attention of the meetings of "the Iron and Steel Institute," and has even been "discussed" at meetings of the Institutions of Civil and Mechanical Engineers.

There is evidently no general answer to the question. Each particular case must be investigated for itself; and M. Gruner has so far generalized the results of experiment and observation hitherto recorded as to give formulas by which the chemical and physical elements of the question may be answered approximately *a priori* (see p. 122 *et seq.*) This answer may be made with sufficient accuracy for practical purposes by ascertaining merely *the proportion of carbonic oxide to carbonic acid* present in the escaping gases of any furnace of which we know the elements of its charges.

The main point of novelty in the Studies, and what gives them their chief interest, is the precision given to this doctrine, first distinctly taught by Mr. Bell, that the ratio of $\frac{CO^2}{CO}$ in the escaping gases is the *index of the working of the furnaces.* The determination of an analytic process of calculation in place of a synthetic is of value for direct investigation of any case of blast furnace working that may present itself.

Still, the other question debated, be it borne in mind, is the economy of *fuel* in furnaces, whether charged into the furnace and consumed there, or supplied from without as caloric in the heated *blast.*

Again, it is only when furnaces are working with the same, or nearly the same, charges of ore, flux, and fuel, *i. e.*, same *quality* of raw materials, and yielding the same quality of iron, that we can get comparative results of a reliable nature. Furnaces may be working in one district as well as in another, although using very different quantities of ore and fuel, and yielding very different quantities of iron, and showing very different profit and loss accounts. Pig-iron making, like other manufactures, must be looked at both from the purely *technical* and the economical point of view. There is a technical maximum of useful effect and an economical maximum of useful effect.

The technical useful effect would be so much the greater as the yield of pig-iron from a given weight of carbon and ores of the poorer qualities is greater, whereas the economical effect often involves other considerations, such as the maximum production of iron of a certain quality regardless of the maximum technical effect. In *most cases*, the iron-master is chiefly interested in the technical effect.

There is however one factor of technical effect, viz., that of the *superheated blast*, which has for the last three years excited the liveliest controversy.

The section 25 of the "Studies" treats of this question on the basis of the experience recorded by Mr. Bell and others in the Transactions of the Iron and Steel Institute, and on the assumption that the *combustible for heating the blast is the gases of the furnace itself.* M. Gruner's examination of the question is, like that of Mr. Bell, full of instructive applications of the actual theory of the blast furnace. The complete technical answer awaits the result of experience of the cost of superheating the blast. To the question, whether there is advantage in heating the blast to 800°, 900°, or 1000°, the theoretical answer is undoubtedly *Yes.* For each rise in temperature of the blast there is increased economy, *abstraction being made, of course, of the cost of maintaining and firing stoves for heating the blast.* At the same time, this economy decreases *rapidly* with the rise in temperature. The economy arising from each accession of 100° to temperature of blast is much less from 800° upwards than from 500° to 700°, and still less than between 400 and 500°, and thus *in practice it is useless* to exceed 700° to 800°. Not having been able to collect sufficient data as to the cost of making and maintaining the stoves for superheating the blast, it is impossible for me to add to the weight of this opinion of M. Gruner, excepting to say that, after examination of all the facts hitherto published, superheated blast beyond the limits safely reached by the cast-iron stoves is useless; and if, as seems to be the case, it be thought necessary to erect *generators of gas to heat brick stoves*, that system is certainly wasteful, and a retrograde step in blast-furnace engineering. This subject is again alluded to in Note V., Appendix.

Some apology is due for writing so much as an Appendix. The truth is, that I examined each subject and factor mentioned in the original text for myself, and conceived it might be useful to others to record my notes for their use.

LEWIS D. B. GORDON.

TOTTERIDGE, September, 1873.

STUDIES OF BLAST FURNACES.

---

§ 1. *Recent modifications in the régime of blast furnaces.*—For several years past the minds of metallurgists have been much preoccupied by two important modifications made in old Blast furnace practice. The furnaces have been increased in *height* and in *diameter*, and the blast is spontaneously heated to a red heat, in England especially, by means of large stoves of fire-brick, prepared by Messrs. Cowper-Siemens, and Mr. Whitwell.

Successive transformations in these two directions have resulted in what is deemed exaggeration by metallurgists, such as Mr. Lowthian Bell, whilst there are others who consider there is no limit save practical possibility. This divergence of opinions has been made known by the publications of the Iron and Steel Institute—an association frequented by Bessemer, Bell, Menelaus, Williams, Snelus, Parry, Siemens, Cochrane, and others well known as leading men in the iron industry of Britain. The question is one well worthy of careful examination and study in reference to the chemical and calorific reactions which come into play in these enormous apparatus. I shall, for this purpose, make use of the series of highly interesting memoirs which Mr. Lowthian Bell has published in the Journal of the Iron and

Steel Institute,* and compare them with my own personal researches on the same subject, some of them given, for many years, in my course of lectures at the *École des Mines* of Paris, and others recently published in the *Recueil des savants étrangers*, and in the *Annales de physique et de chimie.*†

§ 2. *Successive enlargements of blast furnaces.*—Blast furnaces, working with charcoal as fuel, are seldom more than 30 to 35 feet high, nor have they more than 800 to 1200 cubic feet capacity. In Austria, in Russia, and in Sweden, where circumstances admit of a great accumulation of fuel, the height is carried to 45 feet, and the cubic contents to 1800 to 2200 feet. In coal districts the furnaces have been, from the beginning, made larger: and yet the ordinary furnaces of Staffordshire have not more than 2200 to 2500 cubic feet capacity, with a height of 38 to 42 feet; and even the largest do not exceed 3500 to 5000 cubic feet. In 1830, the capacity was not more than 2000 cubic feet as an average, and in Wales 2200 to 2500 cubic feet. In 1860, however, M. Lan and I found that there was a decided tendency to enlargement of the furnaces. In Scotland there were furnaces of 3000 cubic feet, and even 7000 cubic feet; and in Wales the furnaces were of 3000 and up to 5000, with some few as large as 7000 and 7750. These successive enlargements were made with the special object of increasing production, and we were convinced that, in fact, the yield had increased in proportion to the internal capacity.

In the enlarged as in the smaller furnaces in England, the yield was, on the average, a ton of Nos. 1 and 2 iron for 7 to

* Published in one volume complete, with Index, by Messrs. Routledge, in 1872.

† *Savants étrangers*, t. xxii.; *Annales, etc.*, Mai 1872.

8 cubic metres (245 to 280 cubic feet) capacity, a ton of forge iron (gray) Nos. 3 and 4 for 210 to 245 cubic feet, and a ton of mottled forge pig for 175 to 210 cubic feet capacity.

By comparing together a great many Continental furnaces, I had previously arrived at the same results. In my lectures these figures were given as results to be used in determining the dimensions of blast furnaces.

In 1851, the first blast furnace was erected in Cleveland, by Messrs. Bolckow & Vaughan, who built it 42 feet high, and of 4500 cubic feet capacity.

In 1853, Messrs. Bell Brothers founded the Clarence Works, and erected several furnaces 48 feet high, and of 6200 cubic feet capacity.

From 1853 to 1860, a great many furnaces were erected in this district, but none of them were carried to a greater height than 58 feet, with a capacity of 7000 cubic feet, and the greater number were about 50 feet high, with 5200 to 6000 cubic feet capacity.

On the other hand, beginning from 1861, there took place a prodigious enlargement of the furnaces, of which we may give the following examples:—

In 1861, Messrs. Whitwell & Co. built three furnaces at Thornaby 60 feet high, and 13,000 cubic feet capacity.

In 1862, Messrs. Bolckow & Vaughan carried the height to 75 feet, and the capacity to 12,000 cubic feet.

In 1864, Mr. Samuelson built his first furnace, at Newport, 68 feet high and 15,300 cubic feet capacity; and Mr. Thomas Vaughan carried the height to 78 feet, and the capacity to 15,750.

In 1866, Messrs. Bolckow & Vaughan adopted the lofty type of 96 feet, with only 15,000 cubic feet capacity; and

Messrs. Hopkins, Gilkes & Co., at Tees-side, gave 76 feet height, and 20,000 cubic feet capacity.

In 1867, the furnaces at Norton were made 78 feet high, and 26,000 cubic feet.

In 1868, Messrs. Bolckow & Vaughan enlarged their two furnaces of 1866, the one to 26,000 cubic feet, the other to 29,000 cubic feet capacity, the original height being retained —viz., 96 feet.

In 1870, Mr. Cochrane erected a monster furnace at Ormesby, 92 feet high, and 41,000 cubic feet, and at Ferryhill, westward of Middlesborough, with a greater height they combined a smaller capacity—106 feet high, 33,000 cubic feet; and lastly, in 1871, Mr. Cochrane built a furnace 92 feet high, and 42,500 cubic feet capacity.

The internal section of the greater number of these furnaces is given in the plate, copied from the historical account of the gradual development of the blast furnaces in Cleveland, by Mr. J. Gjers.* We see by these that the form is very various—lofty furnaces almost cylindrical alongside of barrels very stumpy, enlarged at the belly, and much contracted at the top. These forms, as well as the height, the total capacity, the mode of charging, etc., have, as we all know, a certain influence in the working of the furnaces. The yield and consumption of raw material vary with these elements. Unfortunately, the short notice of M. Gjers does not give any details on this subject, not even an indication of the maximum yield; but this incompleteness I have, in part at least, been able to supplement by data given in the Memoirs of Mr. Bell, and the reports of the discussions which

* Journal of the Iron and Steel Institute, Nov. 1871.

these Memoirs gave rise to at the meetings of the Iron and Steel Institute.

What strikes us immediately is, that by common consent it is allowed that *the yield of these big furnaces does not increase in the proportion of their capacity.* Thus, at Clarence Works, Mr. Bell's own works, we find, for four types of very different dimensions from each other, yielding forge iron Nos. 3 and 4, the yields as follows:—

Elements of the furnaces.	Old Furnace of 1853.	High Furnace of 1866.	High Furnace of 1865.	High Furnace of 1870.
Total capacity	6000 c. ft.	11,500 c. ft.	15,800 c. ft.	27,000 c. ft.
Height	48 ft.	80 ft.	80 ft.	80 ft.
Production in 24 hours	30 tons.	38·6 tons.	50 tons.	60 tons.
Consumption *of coke* per ton iron	29 cwt.	22½ cwt.	22½ cwt.	22½ cwt.
Internal capacity per ton iron yielded in 24 hours	190 c. ft.	300 c. ft.	330 c. ft.	380 c. ft.

On the other hand, the numerous furnaces of Messrs. Bolckow & Vaughan and those of Ferryhill, in which the same ores and the same coke are used as at Clarence, the blast being heated to the same temperature of 400° C. to 450° C., and the pig being also Nos. 3 and 4, gave the following results:—

Elements of the Furnaces.	Blast Furnaces of Messrs. Bolckow & Vaughan.		Old Furnace at Ferryhill.	New Furnace at Ferryhill.
	Built, 1865.	Built, 1868.		
Total capacity	15,000 c. ft.	25,800 c. ft.	17,000 c. ft.	32,000 c. ft.
Height	95 ft.	95 ft.	80 ft.	80 ft.
Yield in 24 hours	46 tons.	52 tons.	50 tons.	78 tons.
Consumption of coke per ton of pig	22½ cwt.	22½ cwt.	22½ cwt.	20* cwt.
Internal capacity per ton yield in 24 hours	320 c. ft.	490 c. ft.	315 c. ft.	420 c. ft.

* This amount is uncertain.

Lastly, by comparing the three successive types put up by Mr. Samuelson, at Newport, we again found the same figures—

	c. ft.				c. ft.
An old furnace of . .	5000	yields	23 tons in	24 hours =	218 p. ton.
Another furnace, 1864,	15,800	"	45	"	342 "
And the last furnace,	30,300	"	70	"	430 "

Mr. Bell, in the discussions of the Iron and Steel Institute in 1871, affirms, with perfect reason, that he "never found that a furnace of 25,000 cubic feet did twice the work as well as one of half the size."

In fact, we know that in the old furnaces of 5000 cubic feet to 7000 cubic feet capacity, the mean capacity is 210 cubic feet per ton of Nos. 3 and 4 pig, whereas in the more modern furnaces of 10,000 cubic feet to 15,000 cubic feet, we find from 280 to 320 cubic feet capacity per ton of yield, and in the most recent furnaces of 25,000 cubic feet, the capacity per ton of yield is 420 cubic feet to 490 cubic feet. In other words, the descent of the charges requires 60 to 70 hours in the large furnaces, and only 20 to 40 hours in the small ones.

This extreme slowness in the descent of the charges may, in a certain point of view, have advantages. Variations in the raw material are less sensibly felt in the large furnaces. It may also happen that *reduction* goes on under better conditions—that the ore should arrive in the zone of fusion better prepared. But is there no limit to this successive development of the blast furnace? May not the *juste milieu* corresponding to a maximum of economy be overstepped? If the work goes on very slowly, is not the carbonic acid (CO^2), arising from the reduction of the ores, exposed to be converted into carbonic oxide (CO) by contact with incandescent carbon, in proportions increasing as the descent of the charges is slow? In short, is the consumption necessarily so much the less as their dimensions are large, and the descent of the charges slow?

The figures above tabulated answer this question to a certain extent. Previously to 1860, the blast furnaces in Cleveland consumed 1·5 to 1·7 tons of coke for one ton of pig —gray forge—yielded, or, at the very least, 1·45 tons = 29 cwt., according to the statements of Mr. Bell. At present, the consumption in the enlarged furnaces is reduced to 1·125 = 22½ cwt., the blast being heated to 400 to 500 degrees *Centigrade:* but it is quite certain that there is no difference in the consumption of the furnaces of 10,000, 16,000, and 28,000 cubic feet capacity, or even beyond these monstrous dimensions.

If, therefore, beyond a certain limit, the large dimensions produce neither increased yield nor economy of fuel, it does not look very rational to go on increasing the capital for establishing furnaces with these vast dimensions.* This is what has at last occurred to our neighbors on the other (English) side of the Channel. A reaction has taken place in England, at all events in those districts in which the fuel and the ores are liable to crush and compress under their own weight. Thus at Askam-in-Furness, the height has been reduced from 75 feet to 61; at Consett, the furnaces have been reduced from 70 feet to 55; at Workington and at Barrow, situated like Askam in the district of rich hæmatites of Cumberland, the body of the furnaces has, in like manner, been reduced in height—at Workington, from 70

* See note on estimate of cost, Appendix.

feet to 55, and at Barrow, from 75 to 61;* and lastly, at Creusot, a blast furnace which had been raised to 88 feet has likewise been decapitated.

These examples are sufficient to show that a certain height is accompanied by proved inconveniences; but if we desire to appreciate at its true value the influence of these exaggerative dimensions, we must, in the first place, endeavor to form exact notions of the chemical and calorific reactions upon which the working of the blast furnace is based.

§ 3. *Principal reactions in blast furnaces.*—In every furnace of this type, there are two contrary currents in motion, and reacting the one upon the other—a *gaseous current ascending*, the temperature of which is at first very high, and decreases gradually till it quits the furnace at the tunnel-head or top; and a *solid descending current*, composed of the ores, the fluxes, and the fuel, the temperature of which goes on increasing always under the action of the gaseous current in the opposite direction.

Of these two currents the one is slow, the other very rapid. The solid materials of the charges descend rarely with a greater speed than 20 inches *per hour*, whilst the gases pass upwards with a velocity of 20 inches *per second.* Further, the mass of air blown into the furnace is generally greater than that of the solid charges by the tunnel-head in the same time; and the weight of gases going off from the furnace is often more than double that of the melted substances (pig iron and slag) flowing out by the "tap" and slag discharge.

The air, blown into the furnace at the twyres, is almost

* See *Journal of Iron and Steel Institute*, Nov. 1871, p. 409.

instantaneously transformed into carbonic oxide,* and this gas, in its passage up the body of the furnace, acts more or less directly in reducing ores—that is to say, *with* or *without* the aid of the solid carbon.

The reduction of the oxide of iron in the blast furnace may take place in three different ways, according to the portion of the furnace we examine. In general, the oxide of carbon (CO) is transformed into CO^2, which escapes as such by the furnace top without other reaction. In other positions, the CO^2 thus produced becomes again, partially at least, CO by burning solid carbon, which comes in the end, both in its chemical and calorific relations, to be the same thing as if the solid carbon acted directly on the oxygen of the ores, yielding thus either CO^2 or CO.

These three ways of reduction may be represented by the following formulas:—

1. $3CO + Fe^2O^3 = 3CO^2 + 2Fe$;
2. $3C + 2F^2O^3 = 3CO^2 + 4Fe$;
3. $3C + Fe^2O^3 = 3CO + 2Fe$.

It may be at once remarked that the two first ways of reduction are not in fact realizable, if we adopt the propor-

* We know by the experiments of MM. H. Deville and Cailletet, that near the twyres there is a mixture of unconsumed air and of carbon in minute state of subdivision, by the fact of *dissociation*; but higher up, the temperature falls sufficiently to determine the definite combination of carbon and oxygen, in the form of carbonic oxide. As to the question, whether in the first moments CO^2 or CO be produced, it is simply impossible to answer it; and, truth to say, almost idle to discuss it. We may, however, remark, that when carbon is burned on fire bars, the CO is not really produced till the bed of fuel be sufficiently thick to allow of C being taken up; and thus there can be little doubt that carbonic acid is produced in the first place.

tions given in the formulas. In these conditions the metallic iron would be partially reoxidized by the carbonic acid. We know by the experiments of M. Debray, confirmed by Mr. Lowthian Bell, that, in presence of equal volumes of CO and CO^2, peroxide and metallic iron are both brought to the state of *protoxide.* But though these two first modes of reduction are impossible taken singly, they generally help, with the third mode, in producing the final result; and, in fact, the gases taken at the furnace-top are always composed of a mixture of CO and CO^2. According as the one or the other mode of reduction has the greater share in the final result, the proportion of CO or CO^2 in the gases taken at the furnace-top is the greater. But it is easy to show that these three modes of reduction require very different quantities of caloric; and, in this point of view—that is, in reference to the consumption of fuel—it is not a matter of indifference which of these reactions takes place in blast furnaces.

§ 4. *Quantities of caloric absorbed and given off in blast furnaces.*

Let us determine the quantities of caloric *absorbed* and *given off* in the three modes of reduction we have been considering.

The caloric *absorbed* is the same in all three cases:—it is the caloric which a lb. of oxygen would produce in uniting with metallic iron to make peroxide. Let us put C, for the moment, for this number of *calories.* In the first case, the number of calories given off results from the transformation of CO into CO^2. Now each lb. (or other unit of carbon) produces 2403 calories (referred to Centigrade scale and same unit), in talking up $\frac{4}{7}$ lb. of oxygen from the oxide of iron. Hence it follows that for each lb. of oxygen the transformation of CO into CO^2 is accompanied by the giving off of caloric of $\frac{7}{4} \times 2403 = 4205$ calories. Thus the difference ($C - 4025$) represents the calorie required for the reduction of the peroxide of iron under the action of CO passing to the state of CO^2, for each lb. of oxygen taken up.

In the second case, the carbon is transformed into CO^2 by the oxygen of the ore. Under these conditions the lb. of carbon develops 8080 calories in taking up $\frac{8}{3}$ lb. of oxygen, and this gives $\frac{3}{8} \times 8080 = 3030$ cals. for each lb. of oxygen. Consequently $C - 3030$ is the caloric necessary for reduction, when this is effected by the *solid* carbon yielding CO^2.

Lastly, in the third mode of reduction the reaction would be that the oxygen of the ores produced CO directly by means of the solid carbon. But a lb. of *carbon* gives off 2473 calories* when it forms CO: and as it then takes up $\frac{7}{3}$ lb. of oxygen, the caloric given off by each lb. of oxygen is $\frac{3}{7} \times 2473 = 1855$ cals. Consequently the difference $C - 1855$ represents the number of cals. required for reduction when this is effected by solid carbon burning to CO. In order therefore to take up a lb. of oxygen from the peroxide of iron, we have the number of calories given by the following formulas:—

$$C - 4205 \text{ cals.}$$
$$C - 3030 \text{ “}$$
$$C - 1855 \text{ “}$$

* This number, to which we shall have to recur frequently, is determined by the following reasoning. The caloric produced by a lb. of carbon giving CO^2 is evidently equal to the sum of the two results of the transformation of C into CO and then of CO in CO^2. But 1 lb. carbon gives $\frac{7}{3}$ lbs. CO, and as each lb. of CO gives off 2403 cal. in burning, we should have for the $\frac{7}{3}$ lbs. $\frac{7}{3} \times 2403 = 5607$, which leaves for the transformation of C into CO, $8080 - 5607 = 2473$ cals.

The value of C is not rigorously known. It may indeed vary with the physical condition of the peroxide, but it appears to be confined between the limits of 4600 and 4500 calories, so that the first mode of reduction above represented is effected almost without absorption of caloric. Again, and whatever may be the value of C, it is evident that this mode of reduction is much the most favorable, and that the third mode is very disadvantageous. It is therefore of importance that the reduction of the ores in blast furnaces should be effected as far as possible by the first mode only—that is to say, by the CO being transformed into CO^2—or, in other words, *without consumption of solid carbon.* This is what we shall allude to in future as the *ideally perfect* working of a furnace.

When this mode of working is realized, the reactions will be of the simplest kind. The CO produced near the twyres will reduce the ores and be transformed to CO^2, and this in its turn will leave the furnace without reaction on the solid carbon. In this case all the carbon of the charges will pass through the furnace without other alteration than a gradual heating, and this carbon will be finally burned to CO under the action of the blast of the twyres.

To realize this *ideal* working, or at least come as near to it as possible, the reduction must take place in a region of the furnace in which the temperature is relatively feeble, otherwise the CO^2 thus generated will constantly re-form CO at the expense of solid carbon. The furnaces must therefore be sufficiently capacious, or sufficiently high to insure that the whole upper region should remain at this comparatively low temperature; but at the same time the ascent of the gases must be so rapid that it shall remain a very short time in contact with the solid carbon. It is evident besides that ores easily reduced (soft porous ores) will help to realize the *ideal* working more than compact siliceous ores. But, in general, whatever be the ore, the reduction can only take place completely in the hot regions in which the CO^2 will continually get reconverted to CO, and this will be the case more particularly with other oxides than those of iron—such as silica, lime, magnesia, and the oxide of magnesia; the reduc- of these oxides will always require the direct or indirect aid of solid carbon.

§ 5. *The economical working of the furnaces varies with the ratio of* $\frac{CO^2}{CO}$ *in the gases.*—From what precedes it results, that the relative quantities of CO^2 and CO in the gas given off from the furnace depends essentially on the mode of reduction for a given constitution of the charges. And consequently the higher or lower proportions between the two gases will allow of our appreciating the degree of perfection of the working of the blast furnace.*

One or two examples will be sufficient to prove this. We shall see very soon that in the same ironwork, with the same ores, producing the same No. of pig, the temperature of the blast being the same, we find the proportions in the escaping gases as follows, according to the section and dimensions of the furnaces:—

0·3 of the total carbon under the form of			CO^2†
0·7	"	"	CO

* See, for announcement of this fundamental law, section xxxiv. of Mr. Bell's work.

† Abstraction is made here of the CO^2 in the flux. We have at present to do with the products of the *carbon* consumed.

which gives for the proportion $\frac{CO^2}{CO}$ the number 0·673; or, in the case where the working is less economical,

0·2 of the whole carbon in the form CO^2
0·8 " " CO

which gives for $\frac{CO^2}{CO}$ the fraction 0·392.

Let us then now calculate the caloric given off:—

In the first case we have

$$0^{lb}\cdot 3 \times 8080 + 0^{lb}\cdot 7 \times 2473 = 4155 \text{ calories.}$$

In the second,

$$0^{lb}\cdot 2 \times 8080 + 0^{lb}\cdot 8 \times 2473 = 3594 \text{ calories.}$$

Difference, 561 calories.

To obtain the same products, the same quantity of caloric is required. Hence each lb. of carbon burned in the first furnace must be replaced by $1 + \frac{561}{3594} = 1\cdot 155$ in the second, which is, in fact, an increase of from 15 % to 16 %, by the single fact of a smaller production of CO^2, or of the more energetic action which this CO^2 has for the solid carbon in the hot region of the furnace.

Let us now compare a good working furnace with an *ideal* working furnace.

We may take the proportion $\frac{CO^2}{CO} = 0\cdot 673$ as indicating good working.

This is, in fact, the case of the best furnaces in Cleveland, when account is taken of the gases arising from the coke and of those of the flux.

Let us further suppose, as it is actually the case in Cleveland, that for each lb. of pig produced the consumption of pure carbon is 1 lb. and 0^{lb} ·60 of flux. From these data let us first calculate the weight of carbon contained in the gases for each lb. of pig iron.

The coke gives 0·03 of carbon to the pig iron.

On the other hand the 0·60 of lime contains 0·60 × 12 = 0·072 carbon.

It follows that the gases will contain for each lb. of pig produced:—

0^{lb} ·970 the carbon from the coke
0^{lb} ·072 from the limestone

Total, 1^{lb} ·042

But as the proportion above assumed $\frac{CO^2}{CO} = 0·673$ corresponds to 0·3 carbon burned to CO^2 for 0·7 to CO, we shall have, in the gases escaping at the top,

0·3 × 1·042 = 0·3126 of carbon to the state of CO^2
0·7 × 1·042 = 0·7294 " " CO

1·0420

But of the 0^{lb} ·3126 carbon in CO^2, the limestone furnishes 0^{lb} ·072; there remains then as coming from the coke,

0^{lb} ·3126 — 0^{lb} ·072 = 0^{lb} .2406

which gives as the total caloric produced by combustion for each lb. of pig yielded by the furnace—

0·2406 × 8080 = 1944 calories
0·7294 × 2473 = 1804 do.

Total, . 3748 calories.

Now this is the sum of the calories which should be generated in an *ideal* working, in supposing, for greater simplicity, that in the two cases the blast carries in the same number of calories, and that the gases carry off the same dose of sensible heat.

The ideal working supposes that the reduction of the oxide of iron is effected by the CO only, without intervention of solid carbon.

But it is easy to calculate the weight of CO transformed to CO^2 by the reduction of the ores—at least if we take account only of the oxide of iron properly so called. For each lb. of pig iron we have $0^{lb}\cdot97$ iron and $0^{lb}\cdot97 \times \frac{3}{7}$ of oxygen, and this oxygen transforms a weight of CO into CO^2, containing a quantity of carbon equal to $\frac{3}{4}$ of its weight of oxygen.

or $$\frac{3}{4} \times \frac{3}{7} \times 0\cdot97 = 0^{lb}\cdot312.$$

The caloric produced by this carbon in its successive transformation into CO, near the twyres, and into CO^2, in the zone of reduction, is . . $0^{lb}\cdot312 \times 8080 = 2521$ calories.

And thus the CO remaining would have to furnish 1227

Total equal 3748 calories.

But these 1227 calories require $\frac{1227}{2473} = 0^{lb}\cdot496$ of carbon which has been burned near the twyres, and this gives as the final consumption

$$0^{lb}\cdot030 + 0\cdot312 + 0\cdot496 = 0\cdot838 \text{ instead of } 1^{lb\cdot},$$

which, for the case of an ideal working, gives an economy of $0^{lb}\cdot162$ per lb. of pig yielded = 16 %

Let us now show that the proportion $\frac{CO^2}{CO}$ will be, in an *ideally perfect* working, as follows:—

0·312 + 0·072 (from limestone) = 0·384 carbon in CO^2

and . . . . 0·496 " CO,

or total carbon in gas . . . . . 0·8?0.

Hence $$CO^2 = \frac{11}{3} \times 0{\cdot}384 = 1{\cdot}408.$$

$$CO = \frac{7}{3} \times 0{\cdot}496 = 1{\cdot}157$$

therefore . . . . $$\frac{CO^2}{CO} = 1{\cdot}217$$

§ 6. *The ratio* $\frac{CO^2}{CO}$ *is the measure or index of the working of Blast Furnaces.*—It has now been shown by these examples that the ratio $\frac{CO^2}{CO}$ in the escaping gases may vary between wide limits.

In the modern furnaces of Cleveland, the proportion is generally between 0·50 and 0·70 when the working is good; but it is only 0·35 to 0·40 when the furnace is in bad condition. And if we could attain to the *ideal* working, it would be as high as 1·217.

We thus see that this ratio is as it were the *measure* or *index* of the degree of perfection of the working of furnaces. Of a truth, this ratio is found to vary from one district to another, according to the richness of the ores and their quality, the nature and purity of the fuel, the proportion of flux employed, the number of the pig-iron yielded, etc. etc. But in any given ironwork, or in a given district, this ratio will fall or rise,—will recede from or approach to the ideal figure as the furnace works well. It thus appears very important to be able to determine this proportion exactly by experiments easily multiplied. We have already seen by the examples I have quoted that, when the ratio is known, we can easily calculate the absolute quantities of the two gases, and consequently also the sum of the caloric given off by combustion in the blast furnace.

It has been shown above that the direct determination of this ratio allows of our fixing, in a rigorous manner, not only the quantities of CO and CO^2, but also *very approximately* the weight of air for blast and of the escaping gases, and the composition complete of these latter.

§ 7. *Weight and composition of the escaping gases.*—The ordinary or normal working of the blast furnace gives the data of the weight of the flux and of fuel consumed per unit of pig-iron produced. We know also from the quality of the pig yielded the proportion of carbon united to the iron. We may estimate this at 3 % in ordinary forge iron.

Let a the carbon per lb. of pig, b the carbon contained in the flux, and hence p the total carbon in the gases $= a + b - 0{\cdot}03$. If we put y for the weight of CO, and m for the proportion $\frac{CO^2}{CO}$, we have my for the weight of CO^2, and then for determining y we have the equation—

(1.) $$\frac{3}{7}y + \frac{3}{11}my = p$$

which formula expresses that the quantities of carbon in CO and CO^2 are equal to the total carbon in the gases.

Hence we have $$y = \frac{77p}{33 + 21m}.$$

The oxygen contained in the gases will, in like manner, be equal to the oxygen furnished by the blast, and by the charges of ores and flux, which is expressed by the equation—

(2.) $$\frac{4}{7}y + \frac{8}{11}my = d + x$$

in which x represents the oxygen of the blast, and d represents that furnished by the ores and the CO^2 of the flux. From this equation we find

$$x = \frac{y}{77}(64 + 56\,m) - d$$

or

$$x = \left(\frac{44 + 56\,m}{33 + 21\,m}\right)p - d.$$

To calculate x, we must first find the value of d. If *only* the oxide of iron were reduced, it would be easy to determine d exactly. It would be composed of two terms, the oxygen united to b carbon in the CO^2 of the flux, that is $\frac{8}{3}b$; and then the oxygen combined with 0·97 iron or $\frac{3}{7} \times 0{\cdot}97$, if we suppose the iron in the state of peroxide; so that we should have

$$d = \frac{8}{3}b + \frac{3}{7} \times 0{\cdot}97 = \frac{8}{3}b + \frac{2{\cdot}91}{7}$$

But pig-iron generally contains, besides 0·03 of carbon, other elements, such as silicium, manganese, etc. etc., phosphates derived also from the ores. If we knew the composition of the pig-iron, it would be quite as easy to calculate the oxygen derived from these various elements, as of that furnished by the peroxide of iron.

Neglecting this correction, we shall generally get a value of d rather too little, because this would be to suppose that these elements united with as much oxygen as the iron, and *silica* at least gives a much larger proportion.

If we start from an average composition of pig-iron, we shall at all events approximate the truth more nearly, and thus obtain values of d and of x very little different from the true values. Suppose a gray forge pig (Nos. 3 and 4 of English marks). We may admit as its composition, if there be little manganese—

Iron	0·94
Carbon	0·03
Silicium, etc.	0·02
Earthy metals	0·01
	1·00

According to the equivalents, the silica contains 24 of oxygen for 21 silicium, or 8 for 7; the oxygen derived from the silica $= \frac{8}{7}\, 0{\cdot}02$; and this expression would be near the truth if, for a part of the silicium, there were substituted phosphorus and sulphur, for phosphoric acid contains 5O for 4Ph, and sulphuric acid contains 3O for 2S.*

As to the earthy metals, we know that in

Lime, the O corresponds to	$\frac{2}{5}$	metal
Magnesia . . .	$\frac{2}{3}$	"
Alumina . . .	$\frac{6}{7}$	"

We may therefore admit, as an approximate average, $\frac{5}{7}$ of $0^{lb}\cdot01$. At all events, on such a feeble quantity the possible error will be insignificant.

According to the above reasoning the corrected value of the total oxygen in the ore and flux will be—

$$d = \frac{8}{3} b + \frac{3}{7} \times 0{\cdot}94 + \frac{8}{7} \times 0{\cdot}02 + \frac{5}{7} \times 0{\cdot}01$$

$$\text{or } d = \frac{8}{3} b + \frac{1}{7} (2{\cdot}82 + 0{\cdot}16 + 0{\cdot}05) = \frac{8}{3} b + \frac{1}{7} (3{\cdot}03)$$

instead of the former expression, which gave $\frac{8}{3} b + \frac{1}{7} (2{\cdot}91)$.

* Sulphuric acid furnishes for equal weight more oxygen than does silica, but this excess is compensated by the circumstance that the greater part of the sulphur of pig-iron is derived from *sulphurats* and not from sulphates.

The value of d being calculated thus, we can deduce that of x, and we have for the weight of air $4·33x$, and for that of the nitrogen $3·33x$.

But this supposes the air of the blast to be perfectly dry, whilst in reality it is always more or less charged with moisture, which adds, of course, the oxygen of the water to that of the dry air.

The equation $\frac{4}{7}y + \frac{8}{11}my = d + x$, gives therefore for x the oxygen of the air and its moisture united; but it is easy to calculate the values of *dry* air and nitrogen.

It is well known that at the mean temperature of 12° to 13° C = (54° to 56° F), the humidity amounts to about 0·0062 of the weight of dry air, and the oxygen contained $= \frac{8}{9}\,0·0062 = 0·0055$ of the dry air.

Thus if we put z to represent the oxygen derived from dry air and $4·33z$ that of dry air itself, we have—

$$x = z + (0·0055) \times 4·33z = (1 + 0·0238)z$$

and consequently $$z = \frac{x}{1 + 0·0238} = 0·9767x$$

Hence the weight of nitrogen . $= 3·33 \times 0·9767x$

" dry air . $= 4·33 \times 0.9767x$

" moist air $= 1·0062 \times 4·33 + 0·9767x$

$= 4·33 \times 0·9828x.$

In reference to this indirect determination of the mass of air blown through the twyers, it is worth observing, that though it is not rigorously correct, as it depends on a sort of theoretical analysis of the pig-iron, it is nevertheless much more exact than any other mode. It may, of course, be rendered as exact as possible, by ascertaining by proper chemical analysis what is the true composition of the pig-iron.*

§ 8. *Agreement of the formulas with the complete analysis.*—We may conclude from what precedes, that to get the composition of the escaping gases, it is sufficient to determine by experiment the ratio $\frac{CO^2}{CO} = m$. This allows of our calculating exactly the quantities of CO^2 and CO, and very approximately the proportion of nitrogen: and we deduce besides, with the same degree of precision, the weight of blast. All that is neglected is the hydrogen. But in blast-furnaces using coke, the influence of hydrogen is almost nothing. The hydrogen can only come from two sources, the moisture of the air, and the hydro-carburetted gas, which remains in

* The other methods of determining the mass of air are the three following: The first consists in assuming the *ideal* working of the furnaces—that is to say, in supposing that all the carbon of the coke reaches the twyers intact, and then calculating the oxygen corresponding. But we have seen above (Sec. 5) that even in the case of good working the carbon reaching the twyers may be 16 per cent. less than the total carbon of the coke, which, of course, involves an erroneous estimate of the air. The second method, based on the formula for the outflow of air by a conical mouthpiece, gives a still higher figure. This formula, habitually used as given by d'Aubuisson, Karsten, and Weislarch, gives the volume of air which has no other resistance to overcome than the counter-pressure of the atmosphere; whilst, in fact, the blast meets in the furnace a resistance greatly above this, and which no experiments can determine. Besides this, all the air does not pass by the eye of the twyers; a quite notable fraction is thrown back outside. The third method, that based on the volume passed through by the piston of the blowing cylinder, is quite uncertain, because neither the losses by the quantity *thrown back*, above referred to, nor the losses by the *ports and valves*, and in the hot-blast stoves, and from other imperfections, can be determined.

even the best made coke—but this hydrogen is very little, and acts with the CO in reducing the oxide of iron. It also becomes transformed into steam in the upper part of the furnace. Only a small fraction escapes with the gases without being oxidized. Mr. Bell never found more than 0·001 of hydrogen in the gases of Cleveland and Ebelmen, at most, 0·0013 to 0·0018 in the three works of Vienne, Pont-Evêque, and Seraing.

This small proportion has no influence on the working of the furnaces, and may certainly be neglected in the practical calculations with which we are now engaged. There is no question at present of blast-furnaces working with raw coal.

Let us now show how well the formulas we have found correspond with the results found by Mr. Lowthian Bell by two examples:—

Let us take, first, the small furnace of Clarence Works of 1853 (see § 2), the height of which is 48 feet, and the internal capacity 6000 cubic feet. The consumption per ton of iron is 1·45 tons of coke, or 1·318 of pure carbon, and 6·83 of flux.

We have in the formulas of § 17

$$a = 1^{lb}\cdot318$$

$$b = 0\cdot12 \times 0\cdot8 = 0^{lb}\cdot096$$

hence $$p = 1^{lb}\cdot318 + 0\cdot096 - 0\cdot03 = 1^{lb}\cdot384.$$

On the other hand, the analysis of the gases gave

CO^2 . . .	11·80
CO . . .	30·50
Az . . .	57·60
H^2 . . .	0.10
	100·00

and from this we deduce:—

$$\frac{CO^2}{CO} \text{ or } m = \frac{11 \cdot 80}{30.50} = 0 \cdot 387$$

$$CO = y = \frac{77 \times 1 \cdot 384}{33 + 21 \times 0 \cdot 387} = 2^{lb} \cdot 591.$$

$$CO^2 = my = 2 \cdot 591 \times 0 \cdot 387 = 1^{lb} \cdot 002.$$

$$d = \frac{8}{3} \times 0 \cdot 096 + \frac{1}{7}(303) = 0 \cdot 256 + 0 \cdot 423 = 0^{lb} \cdot 679$$

$$x = \frac{2 \cdot 591}{77}(44 + 56 \times 0 \cdot 387) - 0 \cdot 676 = 1^{lb} \cdot 531.$$

$$z = 0 \cdot 9767 \times 1 \cdot 531 = 1^{lb} \cdot 495$$

and the nitrogen $= 3 \cdot 33 \times 1 \cdot 495 = 4^{lb} \cdot 978$,
which gives as the weight of gas per lb. of pig yielded

CO^2 . . .	$1^{lb} \cdot 002$.
CO . . .	$2^{lb} \cdot 591$.
N . . .	$4^{lb} \cdot 978$.
Weight of dry gases	$8^{lb} \cdot 571$.

and Mr. Bell's complete analysis gave

CO^2 .	$1^{lb} \cdot 002$
CO .	$2^{lb} \cdot 591$
N .	$4^{lb} \cdot 893$, a difference of 0.085, or less than 2 %
	$8^{lb} \cdot 486$.

Let us now take, as a second example, the blast furnace of 1866 at Clarence Works, height 80 feet, capacity 11,500 cubic feet. The consumption per lb. of pig is 1·125 lb. of coke = 1·020 of pure carbon, and 0·683 of flux and limestone.

$$a = 1^{lb} \cdot 020$$

$$b = 0^{lb} \cdot 12 \times 0 \cdot 683 = 0 \cdot 082$$

therefore $p = 1^{lb} \cdot 020 + 0 \cdot 082 - 0 \cdot 03 = 1 \cdot 072.$

The analysis of the gases gave

CO^2	. . .	17·30
CO	. . .	25·20
N	. . .	53·40
H	. . .	0·10
		100·00

Hence $\frac{CO^2}{CO}$ or $m = \frac{17{\cdot}3}{25{\cdot}2} = 0{\cdot}6865$

$$CO = y = \frac{77 \times 1{\cdot}072}{33 + 21 \times 0{\cdot}6865} = \frac{82{\cdot}544}{47{\cdot}4165} = 1{\cdot}740.$$

$$CO^2 = my = 1{\cdot}740 \times 0{\cdot}6865 = \ldots\ldots \quad 1{\cdot}195$$

$$d = \frac{8}{3} \times 0{\cdot}082 + \frac{1}{7}(3{\cdot}03) = 0^{lb}{\cdot}219 + 0{\cdot}423 = 0{\cdot}642$$

$$x = \frac{1{\cdot}740}{77}(44 + 56 \times 0{\cdot}6865) - 0{\cdot}642 = 1{\cdot}863 - 0{\cdot}642 = 1^{lb}{\cdot}221$$

$z = 0{\cdot}9767 \times 1{\cdot}221 = 1^{lb}{\cdot}192$

and N $= 3{\cdot}33 \times 1{\cdot}192 = 3^{lb}{\cdot}969.$

which gives the following as the quantities of gas per lb. of pig yielded:—

CO^2	1·195
CO	1·740
N	3·969
weight of dry gases	6·904

and comparing this with the complete analysis—

CO^2 . 1·195

CO . 1·740

N . 3·965, a difference of 0·004 or 0·1 %,

we see thus that the agreement of the formulas is as exact as possible, and indeed, by pure chance, greater than we had any right to expect; for the method of analysis, or rather the method of taking the specimens of gas for analysis, adopted by Mr. Bell, does not admit of perfect exactness.

Although the results given by Mr. Lowthian Bell are the *means* of several specimens, it cannot be admitted that specimens taken almost *instantaneously* really give the true composition of the gas of a blast furnace. Ebelmen himself said, in speaking of the analysis of the gases at Seraing, "We must conclude from this that the analysis of the escaping gas of the furnace does not represent the mean composition of the gaseous current."* And yet Ebelmen looked only to taking the means of the different gaseous currents at a *given instant*, whilst in order to have a clear idea of the working of a blast furnace, not only must we have the exact mean of all the currents escaping at a *given instant*, but of the true mean of a period of several *hours*. This important point has not been realized by any of the apparatus hitherto employed, and in taking specimens the following system is therefore proposed.

§ 9. *A method of taking specimens securing a mean of all the gases during several hours.*

This system is borrowed from the researches of MM. Scheurer-Kestner and Ch. Meunier on the products of combustion of coal.*

In order to obtain an exact mean a certain volume of the total gaseous current which passes from the top of the furnace to the boilers or heating stoves, etc., is drawn off continuously during several hours, and as it would be impracticable

* *Annales des Mines*, t. xix. 4e série, p. 127; also Note I. Appendix.

† *Bulletin de la Société Industrielle de Mulhouse*, 1868.

to collect the totality of the gases thus drawn off, a certain fraction is withdrawn in the same manner and continuously into a Mariotte's jar filled with mercury, containing about 3 *litres.* The general arrangement of the apparatus is as follows:—

Into the main pipe, which carries off the gases, there is passed a copper tube *m n* of 1 centimetre in diameter to 1½ centimetres (a half-inch tube), *fig.* 13, of a length about double the diameter of the main pipe in question. The part inside the main pipe has a slit throughout that length, as at *p. q*, about ½ a millimetre wide ($\frac{1}{50}$ inch). This allows of the gases being drawn uniformly from every part of the current. The part of the copper tube outside the main pipe passes through a refrigerator on Liebig's system. Lastly, the extremity of the tube communicates by means of an India-rubber junction with the leaden pipe which serves as exhaust. This is composed of a kind of trompe *a b*, provided with a cock, which allows of the current of water being regulated, and with a branch *c d* of greater or less length, according to the locality. This latter is soldered to the vertical tube *a b*, a little below the water-cock, and is also provided with a cock, which, working in concert with the other, serves to regulate the flow of gas. It is the end of this branch *c d* which is united to the copper tube *m n* by a joint-piece of India-rubber. Lastly, the lower end of the trompe opens into a cistern of water, which would in fact allow of measuring the gas drawn off by receiving it for a certain number of minutes under a glass receiver.

It might happen in many cases where the pressure of the gases in the main tube is strong that the trompe could be dispensed with, and the gas be taken off at once into the lower cistern without using the current of water. But in any case it is more prudent to provide the trompe. It is a simple means of regulating the flow of the gases. It may be made to come at the rate of three or four litres per minute.

Now, to collect a certain fraction of this gas—two or three litres in the course of several hours—it is only necessary to use the Mariotte vase above mentioned. For this purpose the tube *m n* is provided with a small tube *h* not far from its outer extremity. A bit of India-rubber tubing makes the communication with the straight tube of the Mariotte vase. The flow of mercury is regulated by a bent tube with cock, which may be raised or lowered at pleasure. And then a second upper tube of the Mariotte vase has also a tube with a cock *g*, which is only used when the gas is drawn off for analysis. When the Mariotte vase has to be filled, the mercury must be let in by the vertical tube till it is *full*, and overflows by the cock *g* to expel all air. This cock is then closed, and the mercury rises to the top of the straight tube. Then by means of the India-rubber the connection between this straight tube and the tube *h* of the copper tube *m n* is made. If the gas does not come off spontaneously by the India-rubber, a slight aspiration must be applied so as to expel all air it may contain, and then make the joint with the straight tube of the Mariotte vase.

What has been said above is sufficient to explain the working of the apparatus. It appears that by a double system of aspiration specimens representing as exactly as possible the average of the gases flowing from the furnace during several hours may be taken for analysis. It will of course be well, should the tension at the moment of charging be very different from the general tension, to desist from drawing off the gas until a certain interval has passed, until the usual régime is re-established.

As to the *analysis* of the gases thus collected nothing is more simple, as it is only required to determine the proportions of $\frac{CO^2}{CO}$. It is not necessary to measure or weigh the gas which has to be examined. The way to operate is as follows: The gas comes out slowly by the cock *g* from the Mariotte's vase, by letting in mercury by the straight tube. The gases are dried in U tubes with chloride of calcium, or pumice stone with sulphuric acid. The carbonic acid is taken up by potash tubes. Burn the carbonic acid (CO) by the oxide of copper, retain the water formed by the small quantity of hydrogen present, and then determine the carbonic acid produced from the carbonic oxide by means of a second system of potash tubes. This analysis will only be inaccurate in cases where the gases contain appreciable quantities of carburetted hydrogen, which never takes place when the furnace is working with coke.

A last precaution is perhaps necessary in taking the specimens of gas. There are furnaces which *smoke* a good deal, or in which the gases carry off quantities of fine dust. In such cases the slit in the copper tube might get obstructed more or less. This happened to M. Scheurer-Kestner in his experiments when there was much smoke. This difficulty may be overcome as this able chemist did it. A little *rake*, composed of a short slip of copper put into the copper tube, could be drawn backwards and forwards by a rod passing on the outside, and thus the slit kept clear.

Having determined the ratio $\frac{CO^2}{CO}$, the mean temperature of the gases should be determined. When the mine is not hydrated ores the temperature of the gases may rise to 400° or even 600° C., which renders the mercurial thermometer inapplicable, and there the thermo-electric pyrometer, or the resistance thermometer of Siemens, or the pyrometer of Lamy, based on the variable tensions of CO^2 derived from the decomposition of the carbonates of lime and magnesia.*

§ 10. *Determination of the caloric consumed in Blast Furnaces.* —Suppose we have determined the two elements we have been considering $\frac{CO^2}{CO} = m$, and the temperature of the gases as they leave the furnace. Let us now see how we can employ these elements to determine the working of the furnace. The question is to compare exhaustively the caloric received and the caloric consumed. It has been already shown how the caloric generated in the furnace by combustion may be calculated, when we know the total weight of CO^2 and CO in the escaping gases. Further on it will be shown how the caloric produced near the twyres—in the *zone of fusion*, and that generated in the *zone of reduction*, may be separately estimated. In both cases the caloric carried in by the hot blast must be added to the caloric *produced* in the furnace, in which there is no difficulty if we know the temperature of the blast. It is the sum of these two quantities, caloric produced and caloric thrown in, which makes the total quantity *received*. For the present, let us show how the caloric consumed may be determined.

It is composed of four parts:—

1. The caloric absorbed by the reduction of the ores and

* *Comptes Rendus*, tome lxix. p. 347.

by the fusion of the pig-iron. This is a *constant* element for a given quality of pig, and one which varies very little for different qualities of pig.

2. The caloric absorbed by the fusion of the slags, the decomposition of the limestone, the evaporation of the water in the coke and in the charges of mineral, and lastly, the decomposition of the water in the air.

This second part is essentially variable, not only on account of the different quantities of lime used, and of water in the ore and fluxes, but also from the very varying composition of the slags, which on this account require very different quantities of caloric for their fusion.

3. The sensible heat carried off by the gases. This is also a variable element, but always easily calculated when we know the composition and temperature of the gases.

4. The caloric lost by radiation from the walls of the furnaces by contact, or by artificial means of cooling. Some experiments have been made to determine the losses in this way, but in general they can only be appreciated *by deducting* from the caloric *received* the sum of the quantities due to the first three causes.

Let us now endeavor to estimate the value of these different elements.

§ 11. *Caloric absorbed by the reduction of the ores and the fusion of the pig-iron.*—We may here admit as in § 7 that the pig-iron contains 0·94 of iron, and 0·03 of carbon, and 0·03 of silicium, phosphorus, sulphur, and earthy metals, etc. The caloric absorbed by the *reduction* is equal to that given off by 0·94 iron burned to the state of peroxide, plus the caloric given off by the oxidation of 0·03 silicium, phosphorus, etc.

The caloric produced by the oxidation of iron has been determined by several experimenters.

By burning iron in oxygen Dulong found that the caloric produced for each lb. of oxygen is 4327 calories.*

Supposing there was formed magnetic iron or Fe^3O^4, this would amount per lb. of iron to

$\left(\frac{4 \times 8}{3 \times 28}\right) \times 4327 = \frac{8}{21} \times 4327 =$ 1648 calories,

or, applying the law of *Welther*, for the passage of Fe^3O^4 to Fe^2O^3 per lb. of iron giving *peroxide*, 1854 "

According to Mr. Andrews quoted by Mr. Bell the caloric produced per lb. of iron giving Fe^3O^4 is . . . . 1582 "

and this gives for the *peroxide* . . . . 1780 "

Again, *Favre* and *Silbermann*† found for the transformation of a lb. of iron into protoxide by the wet way was . . . . 1352 "

which gives for the peroxide . . . . . 2028 "

If we adopt the mean of these three determinations we have 1887 calories. This is the figure we shall adopt for the caloric absorbed in the reduction of the peroxide of iron for each lb. of metallic iron yielded. But it must be borne in mind that this number is only a more or less accurate approximation. Not only the experiments quoted do not agree with each other, but we do not know that the law of Welther is exact for the transformation of Fe^3O^4 and FeO into Fe^2O^3; and besides, the quantities of caloric given off and absorbed vary with the density and molecular condition

* *Annales de physique et de chimie*, 3e série, tom. viii.

† *Ibid.*, tom. xxxvii. p. 435.

of the products. Lastly, if we accept the experiments of Despretz, we get a much higher number. According to this physicist the combustion of iron produces 5325 per lb. of oxide, which corresponds to 2019 per lb. of iron passing to the state of Fe^3O^4, and 2271 when the metal is transformed into the peroxide.*

As to the caloric arising from the oxidation of the 0·03 of silicium, phosphorus, earthy metals, etc., it is still more difficult to get accurate data. We know from the experiments of MM. Troost and Hautefeuille, that the caloric produced by the oxidation of silicium is 7830 calories, and according to Mr. Andrews the oxidation of phosphorus yields 5767 calories.

We have no knowledge of the caloric corresponding to the earthy metals. But as silicium is generally the predominant element, we shall not probably be far wrong in adopting 7000 calories for the caloric of each lb. of these elements. It is also probable that the combination of silicium with iron produces caloric, and therefore we may with more confidence reduce the number 7830 calories formed for pure silicium. We may therefore admit that the

* Let us here call to mind that the 1887 calories per lb. *of iron* corresponds to $1887 \times \frac{7}{3} = 4403$ cals. per lb. *of oxygen*. This is the value of C in § 4. It follows hence that the reduction of peroxide of iron by CO is accompanied by slight *absorption* of caloric, $4403 - 4205 = 198$ calories. Whilst if with Mr. Bell we adopt 1780 calories found by Andrews, we have per lb. of oxygen $1780 \times \frac{7}{3} = 4153$ calories, from which would follow that there is a slight *disengagement* of caloric at the moment of reduction by CO, amounting to 52 calories.

reduction of the ores, fluxes, etc., will absorb for each lb. of iron yielded

For the iron proper . .	0· lb. 94 × 1887 =	1774 cals.
For the other elements .	0· lb. 03 × 7000 =	210 "
therefore, the caloric absorbed by the reduction	=	1984 "

And we may at once observe that of these 1984 cals. about 1700 are consumed in the upper part of the furnace, and about 250 to 300 in the lower regions of high temperature. To the caloric of reduction must be added that of the pig-iron in fusion. This is composed of three parts—the caloric absorbed by pig-iron in its passage from ordinary temperatures to that of fusion—the caloric necessary for liquefaction (*the latent heat of fusion*), and lastly, that consumed by the pig-iron in coming to the mean temperature of the hearth.

Practically, however, these distinctions are useless. The essential is to know the *total heat* contained in the pig-iron as it runs from the furnace. This varies with the working of the furnace, and depends essentially on the mean temperature of the hearth, or, in other words, the degree of fusibility of the slags.* If the slags be refractory, such as earthy proto-silicates, the iron will be *hot*, and will run from the tap at a higher temperature than if the slags be rich in manganese and in alkalies—or even if they be bisilicate of two or more bases. We need not therefore be surprised if the estimates of the total caloric of pig-iron, as given by different experimenters, do not agree with each other.

Ordinary calorimeters were employed. The caloric taken up by the water from pig-iron in fusion poured into it was estimated.

* See Note II. Appendix.

M. Minary and Résal, experimenting with pig-iron fused a second time, just before it began to solidify, found 255 cals.* M. Rinman obtained from pig-iron of different brands, 261 cals., 257, 256, 252, and, on the whole, 46 calories would represent the latent heat of fusion.†

Instead of 255, Messrs. Minary and Résal found the total caloric 292 calories, in experimenting with gray foundry iron run from a cupola. But the cast-iron from the blast furnace is generally hotter than that of cupolas. M. Rinman found 300 as a mean for the cast-iron from charcoal furnaces with extremes of 270 and 311.

Messrs. Boulanger and Dulait give‡—

For forge iron—coke furnace .	309 cals.
For foundry iron	337 "

M. Vathaire, on the other hand, found§—

For white iron	280 cals.
For gray, No. 3	330 "

and lastly, Mr. Gillot, civil engineer, found for pig-iron run from a cupola, and as a mean of two experiments made at the blast furnaces of Bizy	337 "

for gray iron from charcoal furnace.

Mr. Bell adopts M. Vathaire's figure, 330 calories: and this is the number we shall adopt for gray No. 3, until better informed. But it is evident that experiments have to be

* *Annales des mines*, 5th series, t. xix. page 406.

† Mémoire présenté à l'Académie de Stockholm, 15th May, 1865.

‡ *Revue de Liége*, 1862, t. ii.

§ Etudes sur les hauts-fourneaux.

multiplied, and especially the dependence of this number, 330, on the greater or less fusibility of the slags, and on the quality of the iron, has to be further examined.

As a résumé, we may in the mean time adopt, as the caloric absorbed by the reduction of the ores, etc., and the fusion of the iron for gray forge iron, No. 3,

	1984 calories for reduction	
and	330 " for fusion	
Total .	2314 calories.	

§ 12. *Caloric absorbed by the fusion of the slag, the decomposition of the limestone, etc.*—The slags have very different degrees of fusibility. Many years ago, Sefström and Berthier ascertained that bisilicates and even trisilicates of lime, magnesia, and alumina, are more fusible than the protosilicates, and generally the most fusible silicates correspond to compositions near to bisilicates.* It is on this account that the bisilicate formula is aimed at in all cases where the presence of sulphur or some analogous motive does not demand an excess of lime in the charges. And from this circumstance we see that not only the caloric absorbed by the slag, but that of the iron yielded, must vary, as above indicated, with the chemical constitution of the slags. The difference in the fusibility of slags has been proved by Plattner also, by comparing it with various alloys of gold and platinum. But if fusibility varies with the composition of the slags, so must the total caloric. The earthy singulosilicates, which are little fusible, must take more caloric than the bisilicates of these bases, or than the silicates containing a certain proportion of alkalies, and of

* See Note II. Appendix.

the oxides of iron and manganese. Hence, a diversity of results has been obtained by experiments on slags as by those on cast-iron.

For a very irony slag from a cupola, MM. Mineray and Résal found 336 calories.

For a slag, approximating to sesquisilicate of lime and of magnesia, M. Rinman found 441 calories, and for another 430. For a glassy slag from charcoal furnace, having manganese in its composition, and approximating to a bisilicate, M. Gillot found 370 to 380 calories.

MM. Dulait and Boulanger found, for a slag of No. 3 iron, 433 calories, and for one from gray iron for foundry, 492.

These two latter slags, like the most of slags coming from blast furnaces working with coke, are generally nearly singulosilicates. The first certainly contained oxide of iron.

Lastly, M. Vathaire found, for a slag from a coke furnace yielding No. 3, 350 calories; and Mr. Bell found even 572 calories, but considers this number as a too high determination. From what precedes, we see that slags which are bisilicates and contain manganese, do not retain more than 370 to 400 calories in flowing from the furnaces, whilst sesquisilicates retain about 450; and that singulosilicates may take as much as 500 calories when they contain neither iron nor manganese, but, on the other hand, a high proportion of earthy bases.

Again, Mr. Bell admits 550 cals. for the total caloric of slags of Cleveland No. 3 iron, by reason of their strong proportion of *lime and alumina.*

In any case, the slags always retain more caloric than the iron. They have both a higher specific heat and a higher latent heat. This latter is as high as 120 cals., according to

Rinman, for sesquisilicates, whilst that of cast-iron is only 46. But we see from the diversity of results, that in order to have an *exact* estimate of the caloric absorbed, we should have to make special experiments on each slag.

We have more exact experiments on the caloric absorbed in the *decomposition of limestone*. MM. Favre and Silbermann found the number 373·5 calories for calcspar, and 360·6 for arragonite.* Thus, in this case again, the molecular state has a certain influence on the caloricity, and it cannot be affirmed that every limestone, crystalline or amorphous, dense or porous, requires the same sum of caloric for its decomposition. Still, we may admit 373·5 for our present purposes.

We have now to estimate the caloric absorbed by the vaporization and decomposition of water. For the evaporation we shall adopt Regnault's number, 606·5 calories.

For the decomposition of water, we have 29,003 calories per lb. of hydrogen set free. This is the caloric produced by the combustion of hydrogen to *steam*.† The result, therefore, is $\frac{29,003}{9} = 3222$ calories per lb. of water.

Let us remark in conclusion, that though the fusion of the slags absorbs caloric, the combination of silica and the bases probably disengages a certain amount of caloric which we cannot estimate.

§ 13. *Sensible heat carried off by the Gases.*—The caloric

* *Annales de physique et de chimie*, 3d series, t. xxxvii.

† 1 lb. hydrogen produces 34,462 calories, the steam being condensed to 0°. If water remained in the state of vapor at 0°, we must deduct 9 + 606·5 = 5458·5. Hence the figure 29,003 above given. Compare *Bell*, section xli. Tr.

carried off by the gases is easily calculated if we know their composition and their temperature.

It is only necessary to consider separately each constituent of the gaseous mixture. Taking the specific heats determined by Regnault we have *per lb.* and *for each degree* Centigrade:—

For CO^2	. .	0·217 calories.
CO	. .	0·226 "
N	. .	0·244 "
Steam	. .	0·480 "

and we find further on, that, according to the mean composition of the gases of blast furnaces (coke), the specific heat is as a general average very nearly 0·237.

§ 14. *Caloric lost by radiation from the walls of furnace, etc.*—The caloric thus lost is composed of several parts. There is the heat carried off by the cooling water, which is easily determined; there is the heat dispersed by radiation from the walls; that which the air carries off in its currents past the walls, and that which passes into the base of the furnace by conduction. These two latter cannot be determined, but we may attempt to determine what is lost by radiation.

Mr. Bell made experiments on this subject on a blast furnace on the Wear. He used an oblong vessel of copper holding about nine quarts of water, every side of which except that put to the furnace was cased with flannel and with wood, with interposed thin strata of air.

By applying this uncovered side to different parts of the wall of the furnace, Mr. Bell ascertained the caloric given off per unit of surface, and hence for the whole surface of the furnace. In this way he found—

For the Wear furnace per lb. of iron .	186	calories
And for the caloric carried off by the water of the twyres, 10,150 lb. of water heated to 9°·16 Centigrade	93	"
Total .	279	"

And to this must be added an allowance for caloric carried off by the air currents, and that lost in the foundations. And thus the number 300 or even 400 calories may be adopted for this source of loss of caloric.

§ 15. *Determination of the Caloric received by a Blast Furnace.*—Let us now return to the caloric produced in the interior of the furnace. Neglecting the caloric resulting from the combination of the elements constituting pig-iron and the slags, the caloric produced is derived solely from the transformation of carbon into a certain mixture of CO^2 and CO.

This caloric may be calculated, either by deduction from the analysis of the gases, or by considering separately the zone of combustion near the twyre and the zone of reduction in which CO is transferred into CO^2.

Let us first apply a knowledge of the analysis of the gases.

Making use of the notation of § 7, we have $y =$ the weight of CO, and $my =$ the weight of CO^2, and hence $\frac{3}{7} y =$ the carbon in CO, and $\frac{3}{11} my =$ the carbon in CO^2. But the carbonic acid contains b of carbon derived from the limestone, therefore the carbonic acid produced by combustion only contains $\left(\frac{3}{11} my - b\right)$ of carbon.

The caloric produced is therefore composed of the two products:—

$$\frac{3}{7}\ y \times 2473 + \left(\frac{3}{11} my - b\right) \times 8080 \text{ calories (4).}$$

Let us now ascertain how this caloric is divided between the two zones. One portion of carbon is transformed into CO in the upper part of the furnace, the remainder descends to the sphere of the twyres, and there again produces CO, and lastly a part of the total CO arising from these two sources is definitively burned to CO^2 by the oxygen of the ores and fluxes. The caloric generated in the zone of *reduction* is thus composed of the sum of the quantities of caloric produced (1) by this partial combustion of carbon into CO in the upper part of the furnace, and (2) by the formation of CO^2 under the action of the ores and fluxes. It is easy to calculate those quantities of caloric respectively.

The 0·94 of iron in a lb. of pig-iron were united in the peroxide to $\frac{3}{7} \times 0{\cdot}94 = 0^{lb}{\cdot}403$ of oxygen, and this oxygen unites with a portion of CO containing $\frac{3}{4} \times 0{\cdot}403 = 0{\cdot}302$ carbon. If, then, the CO^2 thus produced were not partially reconverted to CO, if, in other words, the working of the furnace were what we have termed the *ideal*, we should find in the escaping gases a weight of CO^2 containing $0^{lb}{\cdot}302 + b$ of carbon, b being, as we have said, the weight of carbon in the limestone. But the gases of the furnace contain only $\left(\frac{3}{11} my\right)$ of carbon in CO^2; therefore $0^{lb}{\cdot}302 + b - \left(\frac{3}{11} my\right)$ represents the carbon of the portion of CO^2 which has been reconverted to CO, and as CO^2 burns exactly the weight of carbon which it already possessed, this expression will represent the carbon burned to CO in the region of *reduction*. On the other hand, as $(a - 0{\cdot}03)$ is, according to § 7, the total carbon of the coke, minus the 3 % taken up by the pig-iron, we perceive that the carbon burned at the twyres is given by the difference—

$$(a - 0{\cdot}03) - \left(0{\cdot}302 + b - \frac{3}{11} my \right)$$

and hence the caloric produced near the twyres will be

$$(5) \left\{ (a - 0{\cdot}03) - \left(0{\cdot}302 + b - \frac{3}{11} my \right) \right\} \times 2473 \text{ cals.}$$

As to the caloric *produced in the zone of reduction*, it, as we have seen, arises from

(1) Carbon burned to CO by the ores, or

$$\left(0{\cdot}302 + b - \frac{3}{11} my \right) \times 2473 \text{ calories.} \qquad (6)$$

(2) The CO transformed into CO^2 by the ores.

Now the CO^2 thus formed contains $\left(\frac{3}{11} my - b\right)$ carbon, and corresponds to $\frac{7}{3}\left(\frac{3}{11} my - b\right)$ of CO; (7)

which by combustion would give

$$\frac{7}{3}\left(\frac{3}{11} my - b\right) \times 2403 \text{ calories.}$$

The sum of these three products must equal the number we have found above by the first method—that is, in starting simply from the analysis of the gases—that is, they reproduce the expression—

$$\frac{3}{7} y \times 2473 + \left(\frac{3}{11} my - b\right) \times 8080. \quad (4)$$

And this, in fact, is easily verified. The sum of the two first expressions (5) and (6) come in the first place to

$$(a\ 0{\cdot}03) \times 2473 \text{ calories.}$$

This is the caloric produced by the *total* carbon of the coke transformed to CO. As to the third expression (7), which gives the caloric produced by the transformation of CO^2, it may be written thus—

$$\left(\frac{3}{11} my - b\right) \times \frac{7}{3} \times 2403 = \left(\frac{3}{11} my - b\right) \times 5607;$$

and as $5607 = 8080 - 2473$, we have finally,

$$\frac{7}{3}\left(\frac{3}{11} my - b\right) \times 2403 = \left(\frac{3}{11} my - b\right) \times 8080 - \left(\frac{3}{11} my - b\right) \times$$

2473 and hence the sum of the three expressions (5), (6), and (7) is $\left(a - 0{\cdot}03 - \frac{3}{11} my + b\right) \times 2473 + \frac{3}{11} my - b\Big) \times 8080$ (8)

which is evidently equal to total sum (4); for, according to our notation and equation (1) of § 7, we have

$$a + b - 0^{lb}{\cdot}03 = p$$

and

$$\left(p + \frac{3}{11} my\right) = \frac{3}{7} y$$

so that the coefficient 2473 in the expression (8) becomes $\frac{3}{7} y$ as in the sum (4).

From what we have above said it will now be easy to compare the caloric *consumed* and the caloric *received*. It is sufficient to know for each particular case the ratio $\frac{CO^2}{CO} = m$, and the values of a and b in the charges referred to the lb. of iron yielded.

Let us apply the formulas we have developed to some examples, and first let us take the Cleveland furnaces, which were the subject of Mr. Bell's investigations.

§ 16. *First example.*—As a first example we take the small furnace of Clarence Works of 1853, already mentioned, § 8, and shown in fig. 2. The height is 48 feet and the internal capacity 6000 cubic feet. There are 1·450 tons coke consumed per ton iron yield—that is 1·318 of pure carbon. We have therefore per lb. of iron yielded—

Carbon in the coke, or a = ...	1^{lb} ·318
Carbon in limestone, or b = 0·12 × 0·80	0 ·096
Total carbon	1 ·414
Carbon absorbed by the cast-iron	0 ·030
Total carbon of the gases, or p = .	1^{lb} ·384

According to the analysis of the gases $\frac{CO^2}{CO} = m = 0.387$

These data give, by the formula of § 7, as has been shown in § 8, the following results:—

Weight of the dry Gases.

my or CO^2 = 1^{lb} ·002 Carbon contained 0^{lb}·2735 $= \frac{3}{11} my$

y or CO = 2·591 " 1 ·1105 $= \frac{3}{7} y$.

3·33 = WN = 4·978

Total carbon . 1^{lb} ·3840 = p.

Weight of dry gas = 8·571
Water from coke = 0·051

Weight of moist gas = 8·622

Weight of Air of Blast.

Oxygen of dry air (z) . . .	= 1^{lb} ·495
N	= 4 ·978
Weight of dry air	= 6 ·475
Moisture 0·0062 × 6·473 . .	= 0 ·040
Weight of moist air	= 6^{lb} ·513

or 6·513 *tons* per *ton* of pig-iron yielded.

Caloric carried in by the blast.—The temperature of the blast was 485° C.

The specific heat of dry air is = 0.2375, and as that of vapor is 0·48, the mean specific heat of the blast is

$$\frac{0{\cdot}2375 + 0{\cdot}0062 \times 0{\cdot}40}{1{\cdot}0062} = 0{\cdot}239$$

and this gives, for the caloric carried in by the moist blast, $6{\cdot}513 \times 485° \times 0{\cdot}239 = 755$ calories.

Caloric produced in the furnace.

The caloric due to CO^2—

$$\left(\frac{3}{11} y - b\right) \times 8080 = (0{\cdot}2735 - 0{\cdot}096) \times 8080 = 1434 \text{ calories.}$$

The caloric due to CO—

$$\frac{3}{7} y \times 2473 = 1{\cdot}1105 \times 2473 = \quad . \quad . \quad 2746 \quad \text{“}$$

Caloric produced in the furnace by 1·288
carbon = ... 4180 “
and hence caloric from 1 lb. = . . . 3245 “

whilst, if this lb. were completely burned, it would have produced 8080 calories, so that the caloric really developed is only 0·40 of the calorific power, properly so called, of the coke consumed.

It will now be shown how this caloric *produced* is divided between the zone of the *twyres* and that of *reduction*.

The carbon burned in the zone of reduction is given by the expression,

$$0{\cdot}302 + b - \frac{3}{11} my = 0{\cdot}302 + 0{\cdot}096 - 0{\cdot}2735 = 0^{\text{lb}}{\cdot}1245.$$

The total carbon burned in the furnace, as above shown, is . . . . = 1·288;
therefore, the carbon burned near the twyres . = 1·1635,
and the caloric *produced* in this zone,

$$1{\cdot}1635 \times 2473 = 2877 \text{ calories.}$$

As to the caloric of the zone of reduction, it is composed—(1) of carbon burned to CO, or

$$0{\cdot}1245 \times 2473 = 308 \text{ calories.}$$

(2) of the oxide of carbon

$$\frac{7}{3}\left(\frac{3}{11}my - b\right) = \frac{7}{3}(0{\cdot}1775) = 0{\cdot}414 \text{ calories.}$$

transformed to CO^2

$$\text{or} \quad 0{\cdot}414 \times 2403 = 0{\cdot}995 \text{ calories.}$$

Hence, we have in the zone of reduction,

For carbon burned . .	308	calories.
For CO burned . . .	995	"
Total of zone of reduction	1303	"
Caloric of the zone of twyres	2877	"
Total caloric *produced* .	4180	"
Caloric carried in by the blast	755	"
Total caloric received .	4935	"

Let us now compare with this the total of caloric *absorbed* or utilized by the substances reduced and fused in the furnace.

Referring to § 10, the caloric absorbed may be arranged under four heads:—

(1.) One element, almost constant, which comprises the caloric taken for reduction of the ores and the fusion of the iron, which according to § 11, = 2314 calories.

(2.) The *fusion of the slags*, the *decomposition of the limestone*, etc., § 12.—If we take the data above given, we find—

Fusion of slags . . .	$1·610 \times 550$	= 885 calories.
Decomposition of limestone .	$0·800 \times 373·5$	= 299 "
Evaporation of water in coke	$0·051 \times 606$	= 31 "
Decomposition of vapor in blast	$0·042 \times 3222$	= 129 "
Total		1344 "

(3.) *The caloric carried off by the gases* (§ 13).—The gases escape at the mean temperature of 452° C.; therefore, from the known weight of the gases, we have—

For CO^2 .	$1·002 \times 0·217$	per 1° c.	0·2175 cals.
For CO .	$2·591 \times 0·226$	"	0·5855 "
For N .	$4·978 \times 0·244$	"	1·2146 "
For NO .	$0·051 \times 0·48$	"	0·0245 "
Total of gases	8·622 . . .	"	2·0421 "

and for the mean specific heat of the gases,

$$\frac{2·0421}{8·622} = 0·237,$$

a number which is nearly *constant* in the Cleveland district. Thus, *en résumé*, we find—

(1.) Caloric taken for *reduction* and fusion of the iron	2314 cals.
(2.) Caloric taken for fusion of slags, lime, etc. .	1344 "
(3.) Caloric carried off by the gases . . .	923 "
Total . .	4581 "
and from this we have to deduct as loss by radiation, evection, etc. } difference	358 "
Total, equal to caloric received . =	4935 "

§ 17. *Second example.*—As second example, we take the blast furnace of the Clarence Works of 1866, already mentioned in §§ 2 and 8 (fig. 6).

The elements of this furnace are—height, 80 feet; capacity, 11,500 cubic feet.

Coke consumed per ton	1·125 tons, or pure carbon, 1,020	
Ore	2·240 "	
Limestone . . .	0·683 "	
Slag produced . .	1·520 "	
Temperature of blast . .		485° C.
Temperature of gases . .		332° C.

from which we find per lb. of pig-iron produced,

Carbon of coke, $a =$ . . .	1lb ·020
Carbon of limestone, $b = 0·12 \times 0·683$	0 ·082
Total carbon, $a + b =$ . .	1 ·102
Carbon taken up by iron . .	0 ·030
Total carbon of gases, $p =$.	1lb ·072

On the other hand, the analysis of the gases gave $m =$ 0·6865, which, with use of formulas of § 7, gives the following results:—

Weights of Gases.

my or CO^2 = 1·195	Carbon contained,	$0·326 = \frac{3}{11} my$
y or CO = 1·740	"	$0·746 = \frac{3}{7} y$
$3·33z$ or N = 3·969	"	
	Total carbon .	$1·072 = p.$

Weight of dry gases = 6·904
Water from coke = 0·029

Weight of moist gas = 6·933

Weight of Air in Blast.

Oxygen of dry air (z) . . .	1lb ·192
Nitrogen	3 ·969
Weight of dry air	5 ·161
Moisture 0·0062 × 5·161 . .	0 ·032
Weight of moist air . . .	5lb ·193

or, 5·193 tons per ton of iron made.

Caloric carried in by Blast.

$$5{\cdot}193 \times 485^{\circ} \times 0{\cdot}239 = 602 \text{ calories.}$$

Caloric produced in the Furnace.

Caloric due to CO^2:

$$\left(\frac{3}{11}my - b\right) \times 8080 = (0{\cdot}326 - 0{\cdot}082) \times 8080 = 1971 \text{ cals.}$$

Caloric due to CO:

$$\frac{3}{7}y \times 2473 = 0{\cdot}746 \times 2473 \quad . \quad . \quad . \quad 1845 \text{ “}$$

Caloric produced by 0·990 carbon . . . . 3816 “
and hence caloric by 1 lb. carbon . . . . = 3854 “

Which gives for the caloric really developed 0·48 of the calorific power of the coke consumed.

The 3816 calories divide themselves between the zones of the furnace as follows:—The carbon burned in the zone of reduction is given by the formula:

$$0{\cdot}302 + b - \frac{3}{11}my = 0{\cdot}302 + 0{\cdot}082 - 0{\cdot}326 = 0{\cdot}058.*$$

* It is right to call attention here to this number. 0·058 *absorbed* in transforming CO^2 to CO is *less* than the 0·082 of carbon in the limestone, which proves, contrary to Mr. Bell's opinion, that the whole carbonic acid of the limestone is not necessarily transformed to CO in the blast furnace.

5

Hence the carbon burned *near the twyres* 0·990 — 0·058 = 0·932, and the caloric produced in this region:

$$0{\cdot}932 \times 2743 = 2305 \text{ calories.}$$

The caloric *given off* in the zone of *reduction* arises from

(1.) The carbon burned to CO,

$$= 0{\cdot}058 \times 2473 \quad . \quad . \quad . \quad = 144 \text{ cal.}$$

(2.) The CO burned to CO^2,

$$= \frac{3}{7}\left(\frac{3}{11}my - b\right) \times 2403 = \frac{7}{3} \times 0{\cdot}244 \times 2403 = 1367 \text{ cals.}$$

Caloric produced in zone of reduction . .	1511	"
Or, to sum up, caloric produced near the twyres	2305	cal.
Do. do. zone of reduction . .	1511	
Total caloric produced by combustion . .	3816	cal.
Caloric carried in by the blast	602	cal.
And hence, total caloric *received* . . .	4418	cal.

We can already perceive, by comparing this total of caloric *received* with that of the first example, § 16, that to produce the same *useful effect*, the supply to this second furnace is 517 calories *less*, and the difference is altogether in the caloric of the region of the twyres.

The caloric generated in the zone of *reduction* is even 208 calories *more* in the large furnace than in the small.

Let us now estimate the caloric *absorbed*.

(1.) For the *reduction* of the ores, and the fusion of the pig-iron . . . . 2314 cals.

(2.) For fusion of slag and decomposition of lime-stone, etc., § 12 gives:

Fusion of slags . .	1·510 × 530 = 836 cal.	
Decomposition of lime	0·685 × 373·5 = 255	
Vaporization of water of coke . .	0·029 × 606 = 18	
Decomposition of vapor in blast . . .	0·032 × 3222 = 103	
Together	1212 cal.	1212
Caloric carried in by gases: 6·933 × 332° × 0·237*		545
Total .		4071
And hence loss by radiation and evection (difference)		347
Total of caloric received .		4418 cals.

§ 18. *Third example.*—As third example, we take with Mr. Bell the Ormesby blast furnace, built in 1867 (fig. 8).

The elements of this furnace are:—

Height, 76 feet; capacity, 20,500 c. feet.

As at Clarence Works, the ores smelted are calcined Cleveland ores. The yield is 63 tons of pig, Nos. 3 and 4, in 24 hours, which corresponds to 326 cubic feet capacity per ton of iron:

Coke consumed per ton, 1·100 tons, or of pure carbon, 1·017 t.

Ore	2·440 "
Limestone . . .	0·625 "
Slag produced . .	1·485 "
Temperature of blast	780°
Temperature of gases	412°

* 0·237 is, according to § 16, the *mean* specific heat of the gases.

And from these data we deduce per each lb. of iron yielded:

Carbon of coke, a	$= 1{\cdot}017$
Carbon of limestone, $b = 0{\cdot}12 \times 0{\cdot}625$	$= 0{\cdot}075$
Total carbon, $a + b$ . .	$= 1{\cdot}092$
Carbon absorbed by the pig . . .	$= 0{\cdot}030$
Total carbon in the gases p .	$= 1{\cdot}062$

On the other hand, the analysis of the gases gave $m = 0{\cdot}542$.

With these data, the formulas of § 7 give the following results:—

Weight of Gases.

$$my = CO^2 = 1^{lb}{\cdot}000 \text{ carbon contained } 0^{lb}{\cdot}272 = \frac{3}{11}my.$$

$$y = CO = 1{\cdot}845 \quad \text{do.} \quad \text{do.} \quad 0{\cdot}790 = \frac{3}{7}y.$$

$3{\cdot}33\,z$ or N $= 3{\cdot}745$

Total carbon 1·062.

Weight of dry gases,	$6^{lb}{\cdot}588$
HO from coke .	0 ·028
Weight of moist gas,	6 ·616

Weight of Air in Blast.

Oxygen of the dry air (z) . .	$1^{lb}{\cdot}124$
N.	3 ·743
Weight of dry air . . .	4 ·867
Moisture $0{\cdot}0062 \times 4{\cdot}867$ . .	0 ·030
Weight of moist air . . .	4 ·897

Caloric carried in by Blast.

$4{\cdot}897 \times 780^\circ \times 0{\cdot}239 = 913$ calories.

Caloric produced in the Furnace.

Caloric due to CO^2:

$\left(\frac{3}{11}my - b\right) 8080 = (0^{lb}\cdot 272 - 0\cdot 075) \times 8080 =$. 1592 cals.

Caloric due to CO.

$\frac{3}{7} y \times 2473 = 0\cdot 790 \times 2473$ . . . . . 1954 "

Caloric produced by $1\cdot 062 - 0\cdot 075 = 0^{lb}\cdot 987$ carbon 3546 "

And hence, caloric produced per lb. carbon . . 3593 "

And this gives for the caloric really developed 0·44 of the calorific power of the coke consumed.

These 3546 calories are divided in the following proportions between the two zones of the furnace. The carbon burned in the zone of reduction is given by

$$0\cdot 302 + b - \frac{3}{11} my = 0^{lb}\cdot 302 + 0\cdot 075 - 0\cdot 272 = 0^{lb}\cdot 105$$

Therefore the carbon burned near the twyres $= 0^{lb}\cdot 987 - 0^{lb}\cdot 105 = 0\cdot 882$, and the caloric produced in this region,

$$0\cdot 882 \times 2743 = 2181 \text{ calories.}$$

The caloric generated in the zone of *reduction* arises from

(1.) carbon burned to CO $= 0^{lb}\cdot 105 \times 2473 =$. 260 cals.

(2.) CO transformed to CO^2,

or $\frac{7}{3}\left(\frac{3}{11}my - b\right) \times 2403 = \frac{7}{3} \times 0\cdot 197 \times 2403 =$ 1105 "

	Caloric produced in zone of reduction .	1365 "
Or, *en résumé*,	Caloric produced near twyres .	2181 "
	Caloric from zone of reduction .	1365 "
	Total caloric from combustion	3546 "
	Caloric taken in by blast . .	913 "
	Total caloric *received* by the furnace	4459 "

On the other hand, the caloric *absorbed* is composed of

(1.) That for *reduction* of ore and fusion of pig (a constant) . . . . 2314 cals.

(2.) For fusion of slags, and decomposition of limestone according to § 12.

Fusion slags . .	1·485 × 550 = 817 cals.	
Decomposition of limestone . . .	0·625 × 373·5 = 233	
Evaporation of HO in coke . . .	0·028 × 606 = 17	
Decomposition of vapor in blast . . .	0·030 × 3222 = 97	
	Together . 1164	1164 cals.

(3.) For the sensible heat of gases, $6^{lb} \cdot 616 \times 412^{\circ} \times 0 \cdot 237$ 646

Total . 4124

Hence (4.) loss by radiation and evection (by difference) 335

4459

§ 19. *Fourth example.*—This is the blast furnace at *Consett*, smelting a mixture of calcined Cleveland ores and red hematite of Cumberland.

The elements of the furnace are,

Height 55 feet, capacity 9300 c. ft.

Mean daily yield, 55 tons of pig-iron No. 5, which gives 170 cubic feet capacity per ton yielded.

Coke consumed per ton of iron 1·137 tons, or pure carbon 1.035·5

Ore	2·083
Lime	0·412
Slag produced	0·960
Temperature of blast .	454° C.
Temperature of gas .	677° C.

From these data we have per lb. of pig-iron yielded,

Carbon in coke, a	$= 1^{lb}\cdot0355$
Carbon in limestone, $b = 0\cdot12 \times 0\cdot412$ . .	$= 0\ .0495$
$\therefore a + b$	$= 1\ \cdot0850$
Carbon absorbed by iron	$0\ \cdot0300$
Total carbon in gases, p	$= 1^{lb}\cdot0550$

On the other hand, the analysis of the gases gave $m = 0\cdot502$.

And now, with these data, we have the following results by the formulas of § 7:—

Weight of Gases.

my or $CO^2 = 0^{lb}\cdot9355$ Carbon contained $= 0^{lb}\cdot2555 = \frac{3}{11}my$

y or $CO = 1^{lb}\cdot8655$ do. do. $= 0\ \cdot7995 = \frac{3}{7}y$

Total carbon, $p = 1^{lb}\cdot0550 = p$

$3\cdot33\,z$ or N=	3 ·8760
Weight of dry gases .	6 ·6770
Water from coke . .	0 ·029
Weight of moist gas .	$6^{lb}\cdot706$

Weight of Air in Blast.

Oxygen of dry air (z)	1^{lb} ·164
Nitrogen	3 ·876
Weight of dry air .	5 ·040
Moisture 0·0062 × 5·040	0 ·031
Weight of moist air .	5^{lb} ·071

Caloric carried in by Blast.

$$5{\cdot}071 \times 454^\circ, 5 \times 0{\cdot}239 = 551.$$

Caloric produced in the Furnace.

Caloric due to CO^2

$$\left(\frac{3}{11} my - b\right) \times 8080 = (0{\cdot}2555 - 0{\cdot}0495) \times 8080 = 1664 \text{ cals.}$$

Caloric due to CO.

$$\frac{3}{7} y \times 2673 = 0^{lb}{\cdot}7995 \times 2473 \quad . \quad . \quad . \quad 1977 \text{ “}$$

Caloric produced by 1^{lb} ·0055 of carbon (a — ·03) = 3641 cals.
Therefore, caloric by 1 lb. of carbon . . = 3621 “

Which gives as the caloric really developed 0·45 of the calorific power of the coke consumed.

These 3641 calories are divided between the two zones of the furnace as follows:

The carbon burned in the zone of reduction given by:

$$0{\cdot}302 + b - \frac{3}{11} my = 0^{lb}{\cdot}302 + 0{\cdot}0495 - 0{\cdot}2555 = 0{\cdot}096$$

and therefore the carbon burned near the twyres = 1·0055 — 0^{lb} ·096 = 0·9095, and the caloric produced in this region,

$$0{\cdot}9095 \times 2473 = 2249 \text{ calories.}$$

The caloric generated in the zone of *reduction* arises from

(1.) The carbon burned to CO,

or 0·096 × 2473 . . . . . . 237 cals.

(2.) The CO transformed to CO^2, or

$\frac{7}{3}\left(\frac{3}{11}my - b\right) 2403 = \frac{7}{3} \times 0^{lb}\cdot 206 \times 2403 =$ 1155 "

Caloric produced in the zone of reduction .	1392
Add caloric produced at the twyres . .	2249
Total heat of combustion	3641
Caloric carried in by blast	551
Total caloric *received* by the furnace	4192

On the other hand, the caloric absorbed is composed of,

(1.) reduction of ores and fusion of pig-iron, according to § 11 (constant) . . . . 2314 cals.

(2.) For the fusion of

slags, § 12 .	$0^{lb}\cdot 960 \times 550 =$ 528 cals.	
Decomposition of limestone . .	0·412 × 373·5 = 154	
Evaporation of water of coke .	0·029 × 606 = 18	
Decomposition of HO in air . .	0·031 × 3222 = 100	
Together	800 cals.	800

(3.) For the sensible heat of the gases (§ 13),

$6^{lb}\cdot 706 \times 477^{\circ} \times 0\cdot 237$ . . . . . 758 cals.

Total 3872

(4.) Loss by radiation and evection, etc. (difference) 320

Total equal to the caloric *received* 4192 cals.

§ 20. *Fifth example.*—This is the blast furnace No. 4 of Consett, smelting like the preceding one, a mixture of calcined

Cleveland and red hematite of Cumberland ores. The elements of this furnace are:—

Height 55 feet, and capacity 10,200 c. feet.

The mean yield is 60 tons of Nos. 4 and 5 in 24 hours, or 195 c. feet per ton of pig-iron.

Coke consumed per ton	0·900 ton, or pure carbon 0·819.
Ore	2·083
Limestone . . .	0·406
Slag produced . .	0·950
Temperature of blast	710° C.
Temperature of gases	248° C.

And hence per lb. of pig-iron yielded:—

Carbon of coke, a	$= 0^{lb} \cdot 8190$
Do. of limestone, $b = 0 \cdot 12 \times 0 \cdot 406$	$= 0 \cdot 0485$
Total carbon, $a + b$ . . .	$= 0 \cdot 8675$
Carbon absorbed by iron	$= 0 \cdot 0300$
Total carbon of gases, p .	$= 0^{lb} \cdot 8375$

The analysis of the gases gave $m = 0 \cdot 623$.

Applying the formulas of § 7 we find,

Weight of Gases.

my or $CO^2 = 0 \cdot 8715$ Carbon contained $0 \cdot 2375 = \frac{3}{11} my$.

y or $CO = 1^{lb} \cdot 4000$ do. do. $0 \cdot 6000 = \frac{3}{7} y$.

$3 \cdot 33\, z$ or $N = 2 \cdot 8670$

Total carbon $0 \cdot 8375$

Weight of dry gases	5 ·1385
Water from coke	0 ·0225
Weight of moist gases . .	$5^{lb} \cdot 1610$

Weight of Air in Blast.

Oxygen of dry air (z)	$= 0^{lb}\cdot861$
Nitrogen	$= 2\ \cdot867$
Weight of dry air	$= 3\ \cdot728$
Moisture in air, 0·0062 × 3·728 . . .	$= 0\ \cdot023$
Weight of moist air	$= 3^{lb}\cdot751$

Caloric carried in by Blast.

$$3\cdot751 \times 718^{\circ}\ \text{C.} \times 0\cdot239 = 643 \text{ calories.}$$

Caloric produced in the Blast Furnaces.

Caloric due to CO^2:—

$$\left(\frac{3}{11}my - b\right) \times 8080 = (0\cdot2375 - 0\cdot0485) \times 8080 = 1527 \text{ cals.}$$

Caloric due to CO.

$$\frac{3}{7}y \times 2473 = 0\cdot600 \times 2473 \quad . \quad . \quad . = 1484 \text{ "}$$

Caloric produced by $0^{lb}\cdot789$ of carbon = $(a - 0\cdot03)$ = 3011

Hence caloric produced by 1^{lb}. . . . = 3816

Which gives for the caloric really produced in the furnace 0·47 of the calorific power of the coke consumed.

The 3011 calories are divided as follows between the two zones of the furnace:—

The carbon burned in the zone of *reduction* is

$$0\cdot302 + b - \frac{3}{11}my = 0^{lb}\cdot302 + 0^{lb}\cdot485 - 0^{lb}\cdot2375 = 0\cdot113$$

and therefore the carbon burned near the twyres,

$$0^{lb}\cdot789 - 0\cdot113 = 0\cdot676,$$

and the caloric produced in this region,

$$0\cdot676 \times 2473 = 1672 \text{ cals.}$$

The caloric generated in the zone of reduction arises from

(1.) Carbon burned to CO,
or $0{\cdot}113 \times 2473$ . . . . . . = 279 cals.

(2.) CO transformed into CO^2,
$\frac{7}{3}\left(\frac{3}{11} my - b\right) \times 2403 = \frac{7}{3} \times 0{\cdot}189 \times 2403$ = 1060 "

Caloric produced in the zone of reduction . = 1339 cals.

which, *en résumé*, gives

Caloric produced near the twyres . .	1672 cals.
Do. do. zone of reduction . .	1339
Total caloric of combustion . .	3011
Caloric carried in by the blast . . .	643
Total caloric *received* by the furnace .	3654 cals.

On the other hand, the caloric *absorbed* includes,

(1.) For reduction of ores and fusion of iron (§ 11) constant . . . . 2314 cals.

(2.) For fusion of slags, decomposition of lime, etc., § 12:—

Fusions of slags .	$0{\cdot}950 \times 550$	= 522 cals.	
Decomposition .	$0{\cdot}406 \times 373{\cdot}5$	= 152	
Evaporation of HO in coke . .	$0{\cdot}0225 \times 606$	= 14	
Decomposition of vapor in blast	$0{\cdot}023 \times 3222$	= 74	
Together .		762	762

(3.) For the sensible heat of the gases (§ 13),
$5^{lb}{\cdot}161 \times 248^{\circ} \times 0{\cdot}237$ . . . . . = 303

Total . .	3379 cals.
Hence loss by radiation, evection, etc. (difference)	275
Total equal to caloric *received* .	3654 cals.

§ 21. *Consequences derived from the preceding examples*:—Before applying this method of analysis of the working of blast furnaces to other examples, let us endeavor to extract from the numbers we have arrived at the lessons they teach. Let us examine in turn the influence of the *capacity*, and of the *height*, of the furnaces, and then that of the *temperature of the blast.*

For this purpose we have gathered into a *single table* the most salient results of the examples we have chosen as illustrations.

SYNOPTICAL TABLE OF RESULTS OBTAINED.

Elements of the Furnaces.		Furnace of Clarence Works, 1853.	Furnace of Clarence Works, 1866.	Furnace of Ormesby, 1867.	Furnace of Consett.	Furnace of Consett, No. 4.
Internal capacity of the furnaces	*c. feet*	6000	11,500	20,500	9300	10,200
Height of the furnaces	*feet*	48	80	76	55	55
Yield in 24 hours	*tons*	30	38·6	63	55	60
Capacity per ton yielded in 24 hours	*c. feet*	195	300	320	160	170
Nature of the pig classified by	*Nos.*	3 and 4	3 and 4	3 and 4	5	4 to 4·5
Ore consumed per lb. of pig yielded	*lbs.*	2·440	2·448	2·440	2·083	2·083
Flux consumed per lb. of pig . .	"	0·800	0·683	0·625	0·412	0·406
Total carbon burned	"	1·288	0·990	0·987	1·0055	0·789
Carbon burned in the zone of reduction	"	0·1245	0·058	0·105	0·096	0·113
Temperature of blast . . .	*degs. C.*	485	485	780	454·5	718
Temperature of gases	"	452	332	412	477	248
Value of $m = \frac{CO^2}{CO}$	"	0·387	0·6865	0·542	0·502	0·623
Caloric developed in furnace for each lb. of carbon burned . .	*cals.*	3245	3854	3593	3621	3816
Weight of blast	*lbs.*	6·513	5·193	4·897	5·071	3·751
Weight of gases	"	8·622	6·933	6·616	6·706	5·161
Caloric of combustion in the zone of reduction, per lb. of pig yielded	*cals.*	1303	1511	1365	1392	1339
Caloric of combustion in the zone of the twyres	"	2877	2305	2181	2249	1672
Total *caloric of combustion* . . .	"	4180	3816	3546	3641	3011
Caloric carried in by blast . . .	"	755	602	913	551	643
Total caloric received	"	4935	4418	4459	4192	3654
Caloric of the zone of fusion— Sum of the caloric of combustion near the twyres and that carried in by blast	"	3632	2907	3094	2800	2315
Caloric absorbed by the reduction of the ores and fusion of the iron	"	2314	2314	2314	2314	2314
Caloric absorbed by fusion of slags and decomposition of limestone, etc.	"	1344	1212	1164	800	762
Sensible heat carried off by gases .	"	923	545	646	758	303
Caloric lost by radiation— Radiation from the furnace walls etc. (determined by *difference*)	"	354	367	335	320	275
Sum of the caloric consumed . .	"	4935	4418	4459	4192	3654

Let us remark now, at once, on the subject of the five examples compared in this synoptical table, that the furnaces of Consett are *not rigorously comparable* with the three others. The ores treated are richer—a mixtore of hematites and calcined Cleveland oxides; and, above all, the pig-iron is *cooler*, so to speak—it is Nos. 4 and 5, and not Nos. 3 and 4, like those of Clarence and Ormesby.

On this account we should calculate for Consett furnaces rather less than 330 and 550 calories for the caloric *absorbed* by the fusion of pig and slags. This circumstance explains the relatively feeble amount, found by *difference*, for the caloric lost by the walls, etc., of the furnace at Consett.

Having mentioned this, let us now compare the two furnaces of Clarence, which differ from each other only in capacity and in height, whilst they are charged with exactly the same ores, fluxes, and coke, and with blast at the same temperature, and yield pig-iron of the same quality. If the consumption be different, it must chiefly arise from this difference in capacity and in height in the two furnaces. It is necessary to remark, however, that the section of the furnace of 1866 is more tapering than that of 1853 (figs. 2 and 6). For very different *heights*, the waist of the large furnace is 6 inches more than that of the small one. The distribution of the reducing gases, and consequently the reduction itself, will be *less uniform* in the small furnace, and this circumstance alone may involve a *less economical* working. Nevertheless, we know by the general experience of blast furnaces that this difference of section cannot have any great influence if the mode of charging be suited to the section, which doubtless is the case in Clarence works.

The descent of the charges is slower in the large furnace.

The internal capacity is 300 cubic feet per ton of pig yielded, whereas it is only 195 cubic feet in the small. But this circumstance alone cannot explain the remarkable difference in consumption in the two furnaces. In the greater number of old blast furnaces in Britain and on the Continent, the internal capacity does not exceed 175 to 210 cubic feet, and yet the consumption is often less than in these Cleveland furnaces; and besides, as remarked in § 2, the most modern furnaces of Cleveland, which give 350, 420, and even 500 cubic feet capacity per ton of yield, consume no less—the temperature of blast being the same—than the furnaces of smaller capacity, provided the *height* of these furnaces be suited to the nature of the ores treated, and the temperature of the blast. We have only to consult the numbers referring to Consett furnaces to be convinced that even with heights of 52 feet, and capacities less than 175 cubic feet per ton of yield, we may, with suitable ores, have a very small consumption of fuel; and we therefore already conclude that it would be very rash to assert, in any general terms, that, in all circumstances, blast furnaces of great height and great capacity are necessarily more economical of fuel than those of smaller dimensions.

That which first strikes us, in comparing the two blast furnaces of Clarence, is the difference of temperature of the gases, 452° in the small, against 332° in the large furnace. Then comes the difference in the ratio $\frac{CO^2}{CO}$, which is 0·387 in the small, and 0·6865 in the large.

This low value of m in the small furnace indicates an unfavorable combustion of carbon; that is, an abundant formation of CO at the expense of CO^2 due to the *reduction.*

We see, in fact, that each lb. of carbon burned

produces 3854 calories in the large furnace,
and only 3245 calories in the small.

Difference 609 calories.

We have found, above all, a great difference in the carbon burned in the zone of reduction: 0·058 per lb. of iron in the large furnace, and 0·1245 in the small one; a difference which shows that the small furnace is much further from the ideal working than the large one.

In reality, the *large furnace* consumes per lb. of pig yielded,

1lb ·020 carbon, of which { 0·990 is burned,
0·030 is taken up by the iron.

The *small furnace* consumes

1lb ·318 carbon, of which { 1·288 is burned,
0·030 taken by the iron.

Diff. 0 ·298 in favor of the large furnace.

The synoptical table shows, besides per lb. of pig yielded,

Total caloric *received* by the	*small furnace*	.	4935 cal.
Do. do.	*large furnace*	.	4418
Difference		.	517 cal.

And this excess is supplied partly by the hot blast, partly by combustion, properly so called. Notwithstanding the equality of temperature, the blast carries in more caloric into the small than into the large furnace; because, as it consumes *more* fuel, it requires *more* blast.

The small furnace *receives* from the hot blast	.	755 cal.
The large	.	602
Difference	.	153 cal.

And, on the other hand, the total caloric of *combustion* is

in the small furnace	4180 cal.
in the large	3168
Difference	364 cal.

But what especially characterizes the working of the two furnaces is, that in the higher furnace the caloric directly generated in the region of *reduction* is greater than in the lower furnace; and, on the other hand, it is the lower furnace which receives most caloric near the twyres.

The table gives the following quantities:—

The zone of reduction of the high furnace receives	1511 cal.
Do. do. low furnace receives	1303
Difference	208 cal.
Zone of fusion of the low furnace . . .	3632 cal.
Do. do. high furnace . . .	2907
Difference on other side .	725 cal.

But it is precisely this greater amount of caloric, developed in the zone of reduction, which is the whole advantage of high blast furnaces. In fact, the excess—208 calories—to the profit of the upper region of the large furnace is in no way derived from a greater proportion of *solid carbon* burned in this region. We see, on the contrary, that the carbon consumed in the zone of reduction is only $0^{lb}\cdot058$ in the high furnace, whilst it amounts to $0^{lb}\cdot1245$ in the low. But instead of solid carbon, CO is burned in the zone of reduction of the large furnace. If we refer back to §§ 16 and 17, we find that, per lb. of pig, the quantities of CO transformed to CO^2 are $0^{lb}\cdot414$ in the small, and $\frac{7}{3} \times 0\cdot244 = 0^{lb}\cdot569$ in the large; and the caloric developed in these upper regions is given in the following statement:—

In the Large Furnace.			In the Small Furnace.
By the carbon burned	141 calories	. .	308 calories.
By the CO burned	1367 "	. .	995 "
Total	1511 calories.		1303 calories.

Thus, as already remarked, the large furnace approaches much more nearly to the ideal working than the small one. Less solid carbon is burned, and more CO, and this difference in working is expressed by the difference in the values 0·387 and 0·6865 of the ratio $\frac{CO^2}{CO}$ of the escaping gases. Whilst the gases of the *large furnace* contain, per lb. of pig, 1^{lb}·195 of CO^2 for 1^{lb}·740 of CO, those of the *small* contain 1·002 of CO^2 for 2·591 of CO.

Let us now examine what becomes of the caloric *received* in the two furnaces. We should find in the products, the excess of 517 calories received by the small furnace.

The gases carry off in the form of sensible heat,

923 calories in the small furnace,
and only 545 calories in the large furnace.
Difference 378 calories.

On the other hand, the fusion of the slags, and the decomposition of the limestone, require more caloric in the small furnace, because the excess of *coke* involves an excess of cinder, which, in its turn, requires more lime to flux it. We have, on this account,

1344 calories in the small furnace,
1212 calories in the large furnace.
Difference 132 calories.

The sum of these two differences is 510 calories, leaving only 7 calories of the 517 to account for, and this may well be looked for in the losses by radiation, etc., estimated above by *difference.**

But these 517 calories only represent a feeble proportion of the consumption of the two blast furnaces, that corresponding to the *sensible heat.* There is another much more important, which is indicated by greater proportion of CO in the gases escaping. The gases of the small furnace contain, per lb. of pig, $2^{lb}\cdot 591 - 1^{lb}\cdot 740 = 0^{lb}\cdot 851$ *more* oxide of carbon (CO) than those of the large furnace, which is a difference of calorific power $= 0\cdot 851 \times 2403 = 2045$ calories.

If we add to this the 517 calories of sensible heat, we have 2562 calories *more received* by the small furnace. Of this total, 153 calories come from the hot blast $\therefore 2562 - 153 = 2408$ calories result from the excess of carbon burned; and the weight of the carbon $= \frac{2409}{8080} = 0^{lb}\cdot 298$, which is precisely the difference of consumption of the two furnaces.

We have now analyzed the differences of production and consumption of caloric in the two furnaces. Let us now endeavor to discover the *cause* of these differences.

In the first place, the descent of the charges is much slower in the large furnace. The ore in it does not so soon reach the region where the temperature is sufficiently high to determine the transformation of the CO^2 by the solid carbon of the coke. Quite at the mouth of the furnace the temperature of the gases is higher in the small than in the large furnace—

* The walls of the small furnace, though less in surface, are hotter at top, for the gases have a higher temperature.

452° instead of 332°; and, starting from thence, the temperature must necessarily increase so much the more rapidly, all else being equal, as the tunnel or mouth is nearer the zone of fusion. Mr. Bell found in the 48 feet high furnace,

A cherry red, at . . .	9·7	feet from tunnel.
A bright red (800° to 900°), at .	15·7	"
Temperature of melting copper, at	27·0	"

On the other hand, in the furnace 80 feet high, the bright red was found only at 26 feet below the tunnel, and the point of fusion of copper (1000° to 1200°) 53 feet from tunnel-head. Thus, in the upper part of the large furnace, there is a much more extensive zone in which reduction may go on, as in the *ideal* working, under the action of CO alone, without any consumption of solid carbon.

This is the whole secret of the superiority of the large furnace. For one thing, the gases leave the furnace at a lower temperature, their sensible heat is better utilized, and then, there is a larger proportion of CO^2 formed, which has the great advantage of consuming little solid carbon in the zone of reduction, whilst developing much caloric by the combustion of CO.

But have we the right to conclude from this, that, in a furnace of given dimensions, the consumption will necessarily be so much the less, the slower the charges descend; or, in other words, that by increasing the height and capacity of the furnaces, we shall always effect more economical working?

Is there not, under this double relation of *dimension* and *yield*, some limit? Is there not, as indicated in § 2, a certain rapidity and mean volume giving a maximum of advantages, a sort of *juste milieu*, which cannot be passed with impunity?

It is worth trying to get at the bottom of this question—and first let us examine the case of the small furnaces. What does practical experience say as to the consequences of a very slow descent of the charges.

§ 22. *Influence of extra-slow working.*—Mr. Bell had six blast furnaces at Clarence Works of 48 feet in height, and 6000 cubic feet capacity. The mean of a month's working gave 1·375 tons coke consumed per ton, when the daily yield was 35 tons. This was the normal working of the furnaces. As an experiment, less and less blast was supplied, which gradually reduced the yield; but the consumption is thus recorded,

with a yield of	31·3	tons, the consumption was		1·449	tons.
"	29·4	"	"	1·553	"
"	260·6	"	"	1·717	"

that is to say, *increased consumption by lowering the speed of descent of the charges or rate of working.** This example would not however be conclusive; for even at 26·6 tons per day, the working is not very slow, as for each ton there is only 228 cubic feet of internal capacity.

The following, however, is, in my opinion, a more salient fact. I shall refer to the enormous consumption found by Ebelmen in 1865 in the two small coke furnaces of Pont-Evêque and of Vienne in the Isère.†

At Pont-Evêque a blast furnace of 36 feet high and 1250 cubic feet capacity, produced only 3·6 tons in 24 hours of white forge iron with a consumption of two tons of coke per ton. This was an *extra-slow* working, for the internal capacity was 350 cubic feet per ton of white forge pig.

* See Bell, sect. xxxii. p. 215. † *Annales des Mines*, 4th series. tom. v.

At Vienne, a blast furnace of 33 feet high and 1200 cubic feet capacity yielded 4 tons per day of gray foundry iron, consuming 2·850 tons of coke! In this latter case, however, the working was not so far from the usual working, for the capacity per ton was 310 c. ft. The enormous consumption arose chiefly from the want of height.

Ebelmen was struck by the exaggeration of these figures, but instead of looking for the true cause, he contented himself by drawing the general conclusion, that *blast furnaces working with coke consume twice as much carbon as those working with charcoal*, a perfectly erroneous conclusion.* By reason of the more basic character of the slags, the pig made by coke may require a slight excess of carbon, all being equal. For the great porosity of the charcoal favors its combustion by CO^2 in the upper region of the furnace.†

What we know positively is, that the large consumption in the small furnaces of Pont-Evêque and Vienne arises both from their want of height and the slowness of the descent of the charges. Since 1845 all the furnaces of the Rhone Valley have been carried to heights of 50 and 55 feet; and now the yield is so increased that the internal capacity per ton is not more than 175 to 210 cubic feet; and the consumption is reduced to 1·100 to 1·200 ton of coke per ton of forge pig, when the coke is of good quality, with not more than 10 to 12 per cent. of cinder, etc.

It appears to me then to be ascertained practically that not only a *want of height*, but also an *extra-slow working*, increases the consumption. And theory is in perfect agreement with experience on this head.

* See Note III. Appendix. † Note IV. Appendix.

Whatever be the progress of descent of the charges—whether fast or slow, it is quite evident that their temperature will increase the more rapidly as the height of the furnace is less. Under these conditions, the ore, very little reduced, reaches the zone where the heat is sufficient to burn carbon by the CO^2. Consequently, the consumption must always be great in low furnaces. But there are two extreme cases which would even increase this evil.

If the descent is *too rapid*, in which case the ascending gaseous current has an excess of speed as well as the descending solid current, the oxide of carbon (CO) has not the *time* indispensable for effecting reduction in the upper part of the furnace. If, on the other hand, the descent be *too slow*, the carbonic acid (CO^2), remaining much longer amongst the carbon, will from that circumstance be transformed in larger proportions to CO.

In both cases we diverge from the *ideal* working, we consume more carbon, and we find a less proportion of CO^2 in the gases.*

Consequently, it is quite evident that between these two extremes, there must be for each blast furnace, a *mean speed* of working for which the consumption will be a *minimum*.†

§ 23. *Influence of great height and capacity.*—Let us now consider the immense modern furnaces of Cleveland. Their

* The analyses of Ebelmen give a value of 0·4 for $\frac{CO^2}{CO}$ in the blast furnace of Pont-Evêque, and as the furnace of Vienne gave this value = 0·721, we conclude that the samples did not represent a mean of the currents escaping.

† I do not pretend, be it understood, that this theoretical *minimum* will always be the most favorable practical working. For reducing the *general expenses*, it may be advantageous to force production at the expense of consumption of fuel, though very rarely.

working is relatively slow, for each ton of yield takes 280, 350, and even 420 to 440 cubic feet of capacity.

This slow descent of materials may to a certain extent offer the same inconveniences in these large furnaces as in the small. The CO^2 has time to reform CO, although, owing to the more gradual increase of temperature in the upper region of the large furnaces, this reaction of carbon on CO^2 is much less energetic than in the furnaces of small height. But it is pretty certain that here again there is a *juste milieu* giving a *minimum consumption.*

But it is evident that in reference to the *height* of furnaces it must be limited by the physical qualities of the ore and combustible. If these are small and friable, if they crush or go together under their own weight, it is not possible to exceed a certain height on account of the resistance offered to the passage of the blast, and the uniform ascent of the gases.

And if the *height* be thus limited, it will be the same with the *capacity* of the furnace. It is only by increasing the diameter for a given *height* that the capacity can be increased, and this would render the section too *stumpy*, and consequently, the distribution of the gases irregular and the reduction of the ores partial.

In a word, all the conditions of working would be less favorable. We cannot therefore give excess of capacity any more than we can excess of height. Besides, if the waist of the furnace be large, and the distribution of the currents unequal, this latter inconvenience must be remedied by a slower working. This explains why the monster furnaces of Cleveland have for each ton yielded 300 to 400 cubic feet of capacity, and why also, as soon as it is attempted to work faster, they work less regularly and consume more coke.

We shall now show by some examples that blast furnaces of dimensions beyond certain limits, do not in reality offer any advantages. Take for instance the third furnace mentioned in our table, § 21, that of Ormesby of 1867. It has a height of 76 feet with a capacity of 20,500 cubic feet.

The section (fig. 8) compared with that of Clarence of 1866 (fig. 6) is relatively *stumpy* and swelled out at the waist. Well, notwithstanding its capacity, its almost double yield, it consumes no less fuel than the other, for identically the same ore and the same pig-iron. It gives $0^{lb}\cdot987$ carbon per lb. of pig-iron compared to $0^{lb}\cdot990$, and that notwithstanding a different temperature of blast of 295° (780° — 485°); that is, we have the same consumption, though the one receives 311 calories more by the blast than the other. This clearly indicates a less favorable working, and this is proved by all the figures of the synoptical table.

The value of the ratio $\frac{CO^2}{CO} = m$ is less: 0·542 against 0·6865. The carbon burned in the zone of reduction is greater in amount: $0^{lb}\cdot105$ instead of 0·058. The caloric developed per lb. of carbon is less: 3593 at Ormesby for 3854 calories at Clarence. The gases leave the furnace at a higher temperature, 412° against 332°, and thus the sensible caloric carried off by the gases is 646 calories against 545 at Clarence. The caloric developed in the zone of reduction is less, notwithstanding the excess of carbon burned, 1365 instead of 1511 calories; and finally, although the consumption is almost identical, the total caloric is less in the Ormesby furnace, 3546 against 3816 calories, from which we may conclude that if the higher temperature of blast had not been applied the consumption would have been by so much increased. Thus it seems demonstrated that the large furnace of Ormesby works less economically than that of Clarence Works.

This might be attributed to the *distended* section of the Ormesby furnace. But this section is itself a consequence of the exaggerated capacity, so that we are forced to the conclusion that *beyond a certain limit the enlargement of blast furnaces may not only be no advantage, but may become prejudicial.*

This conclusion is further proved by the following facts, of which the elements are given in Mr. Bell's paper, 32d and 33d sections:—

This distinguished and able iron-master has at Clarence Works several blast furnaces, all of 80 feet in height, but the capacities of which are respectively 11,500, 15,500, and 25,500 cubic feet (§ 2).

But he has been unable to find any appreciable difference between the results furnished by these three types; or rather it is that of the smallest capacity—11,500 cubic feet—the section of which is more *tapering*, which appears to work best; for it is this which approaches the nearest to the *ideal* working.

The proportions of m are as follows:—

Several Furnaces of 11,500 c. ft.	Furnace of 15,500 c. ft.	Furnace of 25,500 c. ft.
$m = 0{\cdot}698$		
$m = 0{\cdot}627$	$m = 0{\cdot}560$	$m = 0{\cdot}637$
$m = 0{\cdot}686$		
Mean $= 0{\cdot}670$		

Mr. Ed. Williams, who manages the Eston Works for Messrs. Bolckow & Vaughan, with furnaces of 15,000, 20,000, and 27,000 cubic feet capacity, all charged with the same charges, and of the uniform height of 95 feet (figs. 7 and 9), asserts, on the other hand, *that he cannot find any advantage in economy or otherwise in the large furnaces.* His long experience has convinced him that beyond the limit of 11,000 to 12,000 cubic feet capacity, the large furnaces of Cleveland really offer no advantage in economy of fuel consumed.

It is also to be observed that the blast furnaces are 15 feet higher than the Clarence furnaces, and yet they burn no less coke, and the temperature of the escaping gases is not lower.

And now, a last remark on the large furnaces of Clarence Works and of Eston.

In § 2 the three types of Clarence and the two huge furnaces of Eston (figs. 7 and 9) of 15,000 and 27,000 cubic feet capacity have been alluded to. These furnaces consume the same weight of coke per ton of pig yielded, 1·125 ton, but this equality is in reality obtained by the much slower working of the large furnaces, which require 420 to 490 cubic feet of capacity per ton of yield in place of 280 to 320 cubic feet. If therefore the large furnaces were made to yield proportionally as much as the smaller furnaces, the consumption of fuel would inevitably be greater, and therefore the working of the monster furnaces is in truth less advantageous. We cannot escape from this alternative, *less production per cubic foot of capacity, or greater consumption of fuel.* This conclusion comes out more strongly from comparison of the two furnaces at Ferryhill already mentioned in § 2.

The one measures 82 feet high, and 16,000 capacity.
The other " 104 " 30,500 "
The first takes 310 c. ft. capacity, the second 420 c. ft.

But, notwithstanding the great difference in height, the

escaping gases have within 6° the same temperature in the 104 feet as in the 82 (191° and 197°), and the consumption of fuel is as nearly as possible the same in the two—1000 tons in the high furnace, and 1025 in the other.*

What is the cause to which we are to attribute this apparent anomaly in blast furnaces in which the gases do not vary in temperature after a certain height, which appears to be from 75 to 80 feet? It is an important question.

§ 24. *Beyond a certain height the temperature of the escaping gases does not diminish by reason of the dissociation of the oxide of carbon.*—We know that the gaseous current of blast furnaces, which at first are composed only of CO and N, become mixed in increasing quantities as they ascend with CO^2, and also with watery vapor when the ores and combustibles are moist, or chemically hydrated. The *reducing* action of the CO is thus partially neutralized in the upper regions of blast furnaces, and we know that certain mixtures of CO^2, CO, and HO have no action on the oxide of iron. Thus M. Debray has proved that the peroxide is simply transformed at intense red heat to protoxide by a mixture of equal volumes of CO and CO^2, and that, on the other hand, this mixture converts metallic iron to this same degree of oxidation. Mr. Bell has verified this double reaction; but this mixture of equal volumes corresponds in weight to

$$m = \frac{CO^2}{CO} = \frac{1{\cdot}829}{0{\cdot}967} = 1{\cdot}581$$

* In one of the last numbers of the *Journal of the Iron and Steel Institute*, that of November 1871, Mr. Bell, recurring to the same subject, thus sums up his conclusions as to the working of the Cleveland furnaces: "After a certain capacity, 15,000 c. ft., for example, the escaping gases are as cool and as rich in CO^2 as those of furnaces of double this capacity" (p. 391). *From discussions of Mr. Samuelson's account of two monster furnaces, read before the Institute of Civil Engineers.*

Whenever, therefore, the CO^2 reaches this proportion, reduction cannot go further than the protoxide, and if the current of gas contains steam as well, reduction would reach its limits even before this proportion, $m = 1{\cdot}581$, was reached.

Besides, there is a certain *time* required—a *prolonged* action of the two gases—to reduce ores in small pieces so long as their temperature is not very high.

But the ores remain only a few hours in the upper regions of the furnaces; consequently they will be little modified by the gases as soon as CO^2 abounds. Thus Mr. Bell has proved that in the Cleveland furnaces, for which the value of m varies between 0·50 and 0·70, reduction almost ceases towards the top of the furnace. At the temperature of melting zinc (about 417°) when the gases contain 31 volumes of CO^2 to 100 CO, which corresponds to $m = 0{\cdot}49$, it requires

5 hours to carry off 1·9 % of the oxygen contained, and
10½ " " 2·9 % " " " *

And when the gases are composed of 50 volumes of CO^2—100 of CO—which gives $m = 0{\cdot}79$, it takes 5½ hours to carry 0·9 % of the oxygen on the ores.

We thus see that even when the gases are *dry and hot*, as in the Cleveland district, reduction at the level of the tunnel is insignificant, and it must therefore be still less when the ores are hydrates or carbonates. And indeed this has been recognized by MM. Ebelmen and Tunner long since. In the experiments at Eisenerz, M. Tunner ascertained that reduction commences when the ratio of $\frac{CO^2}{CO} = 2$, but that metallic

* Section 33 of Mr. Bell's work.

iron does not appear until the ratio descends to 0·70—about 23 feet below the tunnel-head.*

It is however certain that if there were no other chemical reaction in the upper regions of the furnace than the partial reduction of the ores by CO—reduction effected as we know (§ 11) almost without change of temperature—there ought to be some real advantage in increased height of furnace above the point at which the gases still retain a temperature in escaping of 300° to 400°. By such increased height we should inevitably cool the gases more perfectly, and thus utilize more perfectly the caloric produced. But there is another reaction which always takes place in the upper regions of the furnace: this is the dissociation of the carbonic oxide, and it is this transformation of 2 CO into $CO^2 + C$ which, after a certain limit, *prevents the further lowering of the temperature of the gases by any increase of height of the furnace.*

Mr. Bell was the first to point out this singular reaction of the ores on the gases of blast furnaces, and since then I have with much care investigated the principal circumstances attending it. The results of this investigation were communicated to the Academy of Sciences in July, 1871, and the memoir has been published in the *Recueil des savants étrangers*, and in the May number of the *Annales de physique et de chimie* for 1872. I shall here transcribe the conclusions:—

1. If we pass CO over iron ore, heated to 300° to 400°, the oxide of iron is gradually reduced from the surface inwards of each small piece. But from the moment any small portion of the extreme crust of these morsels is brought to the state of metallic iron, the ore cracks in all directions and gets

* Memoir published at Leoben in 1859.

covered with a dust of carbon. This reaction takes place by whatever method the CO is prepared.

2. As the reduction approaches completion the carbon deposit becomes less abundant, and would altogether cease from the moment the oxide of iron (Fe^2O^3) is completely reduced, if this *absolute* reduction could be realized in the conditions under which our experiments were made. But, at all events, this would require a very long time.

3. If we pass CO over metallic iron at the temperature of 300° to 400° C., the iron, in like manner, becomes covered with a dust of carbon from the moment that the reducing action of the CO is *partially tempered* down, whether by the presence of a small proportion of CO^2, or by any source of oxygen which could transform any part of CO into CO^2.

4. On the other hand, CO, pure and dry, gives off so much the less carbon to the metallic iron, as the iron is itself free of all admixture of oxygen, so that there would be scarcely any reduction at 300° or 400°, if the experiment could be made with iron absolutely free of any admixture of oxide.

5. The carbon dust which deposits, either on the ores at the time of their reduction, or on the metallic iron when the CO acts together with a small proportion of CO^2, is a sort of ferruginous carbon—a composition of iron and carbon with 5 % to 7 % of metallic iron as a maximum. This carbon differs from that of steel, or the hexagonal graphite of gray pig-iron.

The ferruginous carbon contains also a small proportion of oxidized iron, chiefly magnetic, the part played by which seems essential in the reaction which determines the deposit of carbon.

6. Carbonic acid acts as an oxidizing agent on iron; but

at the temperature of 300° to 400° the action is not intense. There is only a small quantity produced in variable proportions of Fe^2O^3, Fe^2O^3 + FeO, and FeO; that is to say, of the peroxide, the magnetic oxide, and the protoxide of iron, and these oxides are never accompanied by a deposit of carbon.

7. The formation of ferruginous carbon is the result of a sort of dissociation of CO. 2CO is transformed to CO^2 + C, but this reaction never takes place *directly*. That it may take place there must be simultaneous presence of *metallic iron and protoxide of iron*—the metallic iron to fix the carbon, the protoxide to retain for a moment the oxygen.

But this passing reoxidation of the protoxide, which resists its final reduction by this very reaction, can only be produced if the reducing action of the CO be *partially tempered down* by CO^2. This, I repeat, is the *sine qua non* condition of the deposit of carbon. This double reaction is expressed by the formulas—

$$3FeO + CO = Fe^3O^4 + C$$

(this carbon having been united to the iron),

and $$Fe^3O^4 + CO = 3FeO + CO,$$

and so on indefinitely, provided that the CO is always *tempered* in reductive action by a certain portion of CO^2. In one word, CO pure is not dissociated by iron absolutely free from an oxidized element. In the same way, CO^2, if it acts alone on iron, does not deposit ferruginous carbon; and lastly, the two gases united, provided CO be in excess, produce an abundance of ferruginous carbon by the simultaneous action on metallic iron at the low temperature of 300° to 400°.

8. Spathore iron, or the protoxide of iron (FeO), is rapidly

transformed into magnetic oxide under the action of CO^2 without any deposit of carbon, whilst CO in the same circumstances rapidly deposits large quantities of ferruginous carbon.

9. If we raise the temperature to a lively red, in those experiments which give ferruginous carbon, the deposit immediately ceases, and, moreover, the carbon already deposited is burned again so long as there is present a sufficient quantity of oxide unreduced.

Thus the reactions are in this respect quite different at high temperatures from what they are at temperatures of 300° to 400°.

10. In reference to the theory of the blast furnace, it may be remarked that the carbon must deposit itself on the ores in the upper regions of the furnace, and that this carbon dust must facilitate the ulterior reduction of the ores, and that of CO^2, in the middle regions of the furnace.

At all events, in consequence of this reaction, the carbon deposited will be burned a second time in the zone of fusion.

11. The dissociation of CO takes place with a development of caloric. For each unit of carbon deposited there is a disengagement of 3134 calories.

To the *résumé* of what goes before, I add two observations. The dissociation of CO does not take place when a mixture of *equal volumes* of CO and CO^2 are made to act on the oxide of iron, that is when $m = 1{\cdot}581$. According to M. Debray's experiments, only FeO is formed in this case, whilst metallic iron is *necessary* to determine the deposit of carbon dust. If, on the other hand, we have 2 *vols. CO to* 1 *vol.* CO^2, which corresponds to $m = {\cdot}79$, then the carbon commences to deposit, for then also metallic iron begins to appear, provided of course that the current of gases be sufficiently rapid to carry off, without delay, the CO^2 formed.

My second observation is relative to the disengagement of 3134 calories, due to the deposit of ferruginous carbon. This is the essential point of the phenomenon in question, as regards the temperature of the gases and the limit of height of blast furnaces. The caloric produced by the combustion of 2 C to 2 CO is, as we know, $2 \times 2473 = 4946$ calories. On the other hand, when the half of 2 C is transformed into CO^2, the caloric developed is 8080 calories: therefore the dissociation of 2 CO into $C + CO^2$ unquestionably sets free $8080 - 4946 = 3134$ calories.

We may therefore conclude that when the escaping gases have a temperature of 300° to 400°, and such a composition that the ratio $m = \frac{CO^2}{CO} = 0{\cdot}80$, there will be not only partial reduction of the ores, but also *impregnation and deposit of carbon dust*, with a notable disengagement of caloric, from which there results a sort of stationary condition without any further lowering of temperature of the gases, notwithstanding greater height given to furnace.

But what actually takes place is this:—

In the upper part of the furnaces, two different reactions take place at the same time. On the one hand, ore is reduced by CO giving CO^2 without sensible change of temperature. On the other hand, 2 CO is transformed to $C + CO^2$, with a production of 3136 calories. The carbon C resulting from this dissociation is restored to the charge in the shape of carbon dust. It descends with the charge, and then reforms CO in the lower hotter regions. The CO thus reproduced ascends again, and is dissociated in its turn into ($\frac{1}{2}$ C + $\frac{1}{2}$ CO^2).

And the same reaction is renewed indefinitely, and thus the sum of the reactions is just as if the 2 CO had been directly transformed into 2 CO^2 by the oxygen of the ores; that is, as if the reduction took place, as assumed in the *ideal* working, by the action of CO without consumption of solid carbon, and consequently without sensible variation of temperature.

The dissociation of the CO brings the ordinary good working nearly up to the *ideal working*, and consequently whatever favors this *dissociation* will reduce the consumption of fuel; and hence we may conclude increase of height of furnaces would lead to a gradual diminution of consumption, the extreme limit of which would be the *ideal working* of the furnace.

But, in fact, this could not be realized. In the first place, the height of the furnaces is limited by the increasing resistance of the charges to the passage of the blast. Again, although the *sum* total of the caloric disengaged depends solely on the value of the ratio *m* for a given consumption, its *distribution* will be chiefly regulated by the *manner* of production of CO^2. When CO^2 comes from the dissociation of 2 CO, there is *production of caloric* in the upper region of the furnace, whilst there would be *absorption* in the *middle* region where the carbon desposited is transformed into CO by the oxygen of the ore. It is true that there is only a *displacement* of caloric, but the gases thus reheated in the upper part of the furnace will, from want of time, yield less caloric to the cold elements of the charges than if their temperature had been raised in the middle regions by the simple oxidation of CO to CO^2 by the ores.

Raising the height of furnaces tends to a sort of *constant* calorific state *by favoring the dissociation of CO*, but after this there can be no sensible advantage.

I shall only add one more observation. All that I have said applies only to blast furnaces in which *calcined* anhydrous ores alone are charged, as in Cleveland. Elsewhere, in the districts of France where hydrated oxides are used, for example, and in districts also where incompletely calcined spathic ores are used, the tunnel-head is much cooler. Thus I have quoted from M. Tunner's memoir the example of Eisenerz, where the metallic iron, and with it the dissociation of CO, does not begin to declare itself till 23 feet below the top. But in furnaces of small height, the charges would get into the highly heated zones in which this reaction ceases again very soon after. Any raising of the height of furnaces, in such cases, might enlarge the zone in which dissociation would take place, and thus lead finally to a certain economy by rendering the gases richer in CO^2. But it is evident, for the reasons above given, that there is here again a limit at which real economy becomes insignificant.—*En résumé*—

After a certain height has been attained, variable with the ores and the section of the furnaces, there is no longer any advantage in enlarging their capacity.

§ 25. *Influence of highly heated blast.*—Let us now, in the second place, *endeavor to appreciate the influence of variations of the temperature of the blast on the working of the furnace.*

Let us, for this purpose, compare the two furnaces of Consett, cited in our synoptical table.

The dimensions and the section differ very little; the charges are identical; the pig-iron yielded is the same. On the other hand, the temperature of the blast is 454°·5 in the one, and 718° in the other. The difference in the results obtained can therefore only be attributed to the difference of 263° of temperature. The blast of the one furnace is heated in ordinary cast-metal tubes, that of the other in one of Whitwell's brick stoves. The combustible for heating is, in both cases, the furnace gases.

What strikes us at once is, that the escaping gases are colder, the hotter the blast—viz., 477° for the 454° blast, against 248° for the 718° blast. This is indeed a well-known, well-ascertained result wherever hot-blast is substituted for cold. The hot-blast *cools the top of the furnace*, because a larger proportion of the caloric *received* is due to the blast. Combustion furnishes less gas, and this is better cooled in ascending through the same mass of solid materials.

The differences between the two Consett furnaces are great in these points of view.

The furnace with highly heated blast receives per lb. of iron yielded, only . . . . 3^{lb}·751 blast,
and gives off only . . . . . . 5^{lb}·161 of gases,
whilst the furnace with blast at *ordinary* temperature of hot blast, *receives* . . 5^{lb}·071 of blast,
and gives off . . . . 6^{lb}·706 of gases.

The caloric of combustion in the zone of twyres is 1672 calories only in the first case, against 2249 calories in the second, and this enormous difference is only compensated in a very small degree by the caloric carried in by the blast, which is 643 calories against 551 calories—a difference of 92 calories. Again, the zone of fusion of the furnace with ordinary hot blast, receives, notwithstanding this, an excess of caloric of

$$2800 - 2315 = 485 \text{ calories,}$$

and the difference is still greater in the total caloric received by the two furnaces; this is

$$4192 - 3654 = 538 \text{ calories.}$$

But this excess of caloric *received* by the furnace with ordinary hot blast is accounted for almost wholly by the caloric carried off by the gases, which amounts to 758 calories in the first furnace, against 303 calories carried off by the gases of furnace with highly heated blast. Difference, 455 calories.

The advantages of the superheated blast are manifested by the higher ratio of $\frac{CO^2}{CO} = m$, which is 0·623, instead of 0·502. The carbon burned is better utilized; and this difference certainly arises from the lower temperature of the zone of reduction tending to determine a more active dissociation of the CO.

Thus, the use of *superheated blast* at Consett gives an economy of $1^{lb}\cdot0055 - 0^{lb}\cdot789 = 0^{lb}\cdot2165$ carbon (pure) per lb. of iron yielded—an economy of which only a very small amount arises from the caloric carried in directly by the *superheated* blast.* It is chiefly due to more useful *distribution* of the caloric which effects a more energetic cooling of the gases, and to the earlier combustion of the carbon developing 3816 calories per lb. in the case of superheated blast, and 3621 calories in the case of ordinary hot-blast.

Thus, there are considerable advantages obtained by the superheating of the blasts to the extent we have been

* The excess of caloric carried in by the superheated blast is 92 calories, and this replaces only $\frac{92}{2473} = 0\cdot037$ of carbon burned at the twyres.

examining, and that without any alteration in the nature of the products obtained, when working with ordinary ores.

It remains to be seen whether, in reference to this question, there are not other limits besides practical possibility.

Might we without prejudice heat the blast to 800°, 900°, 1000°, etc., and will each increment of temperature be accompanied by an equivalent economy in the carbon consumed?

Experience alone can solve this problem. But from the facts we have collected, we can, to a certain extent, ascertain what would be the result of further heating the *blast.*

As the temperature of the blast increases, the temperature at the tunnel-head decreases. This is a fact well ascertained, and the Consett experience proves it once more. The hot blast acts, in this respect, like an increased height of furnace; but the dissociation of the CO puts a limit to this cooling.

According to the results given by the highest furnace of Cleveland, it appears that the temperature of the escaping gases does not descend below 200° C. I speak always, of course, of furnaces supplied with calcined Cleveland ores, and not of furnaces smelting hydrated or carbonated ores.

At the highest furnace of Cleveland, that of Ferryhill of 104 feet high, the gases have still a temperature of 191° C.; and yet in these works they use in the charges ores which travel 40 miles *after* their calcination, which in ordinary circumstances must give rise to the absorption of a certain amount of humidity. We may therefore admit as the lower limit, in Cleveland conditions, a temperature of 200° C. at the tunnel-head.

Another consequence of the use of highly heated blast, as of the increased height of the furnace, is the gradual increase in the value of m. We approximate to the *ideal* working, and we have seen that at Consett the ratio m rises from 0·502 to 0·623. As the blast is more heated the combustion of carbon at the twyres decreases, and therefore the mass of CO produced above this point diminishes. But, as the oxygen of the ore is constant, there must take place one of two things—either the CO^2 will go on increasing, and the limit at which the CO *dissociates* will soon be reached, which corresponds to $m = 0·80$, and soon after the ideal working would be reached, where $m = 1·217$ (§ 5); or the excess of CO^2 in the region of reduction will act on the solid carbon, and, while the consumption near the twyres will decrease, it will increase in the region of reduction—or, rather, in general, the two effects will be simultaneous;—the ratio m will be seen to increase concurrently with quantity of carbon burned in the region of reduction. This is exactly what takes place at Consett. In comparing the furnace with ordinary hot blast and that with superheated blast, we see that not only m passes from 0·502 to 0·623, but the carbon burned in the zone of reduction rises from 0·096 to 0·113. Now, starting from the consumption at Consett, we can easily calculate, for quantities of carbon burned at the twyres successively decreasing, and values of m successively increasing, the temperatures that must be given to the blast, and also the carbon burned in the zone of reduction.

I shall first assume a constant value of $m = 0·623$, the figure found for Consett furnace working with blast at 718° C.

We have seen that in this case the carbon burned at the level of the twyres is $0^{lb}·789 - 0·113 = 0^{lb}·676$. Let us suppose this weight reduced successively to 0·650 and 0·600. Let us calculate the carbon burned in the zone of reduction under these conditions, and let us determine what must be the temperature of the blast to get the caloric *necessary* for the working of the furnace.

We know the total oxygen supplied to the gases of the furnace. It is composed of the oxygen derived from the charge, and of that carried in by the blast. But this sum should equal the total oxygen of the carbonic oxide and the carbonic acid of the gases, that is to say, $= \frac{4}{7} y + \frac{8}{11} my$, according to the notation of § 7. This ratio will allow of our determining the values of y and my, and consequently the total carbon contained in the gases.

The oxygen of the charge is given by formula (3.) § 7,

$$d = \frac{8}{3} b + \frac{1}{7} (3{\cdot}03)$$

but it is well to remark that the term $\frac{1}{7}$ (3·03), which represents the oxygen of the ore, is composed of two parts, the oxygen abandoned in the zone of reduction $= \frac{1}{7}$ (2·82) = 0^{lb}·403, and the oxygen taken up near the twyres by the direct action of the carbon $= \frac{1}{7}$ (0·21) = 0·030.*

The oxygen carried in by the blast is determined by the carbon burned near the twyres. But one of carbon combines with $\frac{4}{3}$ of oxygen to form CO: if then the weight of carbon be 0·650, we shall have for corresponding oxygen $\frac{4}{3} \times 0{\cdot}650 =$ 0·867, of which 0·030 is furnished by the charge, and 0·837 by the blast.

Let us apply these principles to the furnaces of Consett No. 4 (§ 20), in which the carbon of the limestone $b = 0{\cdot}0485$ we shall have for total *oxygen*,

* See § 7, p. 36 *ante*.

$$0^{lb}\cdot867 + 0^{lb}\cdot403 + \frac{8}{3}(0^{lb}\cdot0485) = 1^{lb}\cdot399,$$

and consequently we have the equation,

$$\frac{4}{7}y + \frac{8}{11}my = 1^{lb}\cdot399,$$

or, as $m = 0\cdot623$,

$$\left(\frac{4}{7} = \frac{8}{11} \times 0\cdot623\right)y = 1^{lb}\cdot399.$$

$$\text{And hence CO or } y = \frac{77 \times 1\cdot399}{44 + 56 \times 0\cdot623} = 1\cdot365$$

$$CO^2 = my = 0\cdot623 \times 0\cdot625 = 0\cdot850$$

But the CO or y contains . $\frac{3}{7} \times 1\cdot365 = 0\cdot585$ carbon.

And the CO^2 or my " . $\frac{3}{11} \times 0\cdot850 = 0\cdot232$ "

or the total carbon of the gases, p, . . $0\cdot817$ "

and as the carbon burned at the twyre and that supplied by the limestone are $= 0\cdot650 + 0.0485$ . . . . . . $= 0\cdot6985$ "

we have for the carbon burned in the zone of reduction . . . . . . $0\cdot1185$ "

And now from the total carbon we can deduce the caloric of combustion :—

The CO develops . . .	$0\cdot585 \times 2473 =$	1446 cal.
The CO^2 gives .	$(0\cdot232 — 0\cdot0485) \times 8080 =$	1483
	Total caloric of combustion	2929 cal.

Let us admit that the caloric absorbed is the same as was ascertained for No. 4 furnace at Consett (§ 20), *i. e.* 3654 cals., the blast must therefore carry in 725 cals. instead of 643.

But in reality the caloric absorbed will be *less*, because the *weight of the gases will be less*, and besides, their temperature would be somewhat lowered. We should find for this difference a maximum value, by supposing that we get to the limit of cooling at 200°, above indicated.

The weight of the gases is as follows:—

my or CO^2	$= 0{\cdot}850$	
y or CO	$= 1{\cdot}365$	
N $3{\cdot}33 \times 0{\cdot}837 \times 0{\cdot}9767$	$= 2{\cdot}722$	The oxygen *x* of blast being $= 0{\cdot}837$
Weight of dry air .	$4{\cdot}937$	
Water from coke . .	$0{\cdot}022$	
Weight of moist gases .	$4{\cdot}959$	instead of $5{\cdot}161$ of § 20.

Therefore the caloric carried off by the gases will be

$$4^{\text{lb}}{\cdot}959 \times 200^\circ \times 0{\cdot}237 = 235 \text{ calories,}$$

instead of 303 calories found in § 20. The caloric *absorbed* or *necessary* will therefore be decreased by 68 calories, and thus reduced from 3654 to 3586.

Although in fact the gases would escape at a somewhat higher temperature than 200°, let us admit these numbers.

The blast would have to furnish *at least*

$$3586 - 2929 = 657 \text{ calories,}$$

and as the weight of blast is, according to the formulas of § 7,

$$0{\cdot}857 \times 4{\cdot}33 \times 0{\cdot}9828 = 3^{\text{lb}}{\cdot}562,$$

we then have for the minimum *temperature of the blast*,

$$\frac{657}{3{\cdot}562 \times 0{\cdot}239} = \frac{657}{0{\cdot}851} = 772^\circ.$$

Let us now calculate the caloric developed in the zone of reduction. It is equal to the total caloric of combustion

minus the caloric developed near the twyres by the combustion of 0·650 of carbon, which is . 0·650 × 2473 = 1607 cals.
and there therefore remains for the caloric of the
zone of reduction 1322

Total calories, as above 2929

But, according to the synoptical table of § 21, the caloric of combustion in the zone of reduction of No. 4 Consett furnace is 1339 calories. Thus, as has been already remarked, as the temperature of the *blast increases* the caloric of combustion *diminishes* in the zone of reduction, and that notwithstanding the increase of the carbon consumed in this region, which rises in this case from 0·113 to 0·1185.

Let us now go through the same calculations for the case in which the carbon consumed near the twyres is reduced to $0^{lb}\cdot600$.

The oxygen corresponding $= \frac{4}{3} \times 0\cdot600 = 0\cdot800$, and as 0·030 is furnished by the charge, there remains for the blast 0·770, and hence the total oxygen will be,

$$0\cdot800 + 0\cdot403 + \frac{8}{3}(0\cdot0485) = 1^{lb}\cdot332,$$

which gives

$$CO = y = \frac{77 \times 1\cdot332}{78\cdot08} = 1\cdot300 \text{ containing carbon, } 0\cdot557$$

and $CO^2 = my = 1\cdot300 \times 0\cdot623 = 0\cdot810$, . . . 0·221

Total carbon of gases, 0·778

Carbon burned at twyres and derived from limestone, 0·6485

Therefore carbon burned in zone of reduction, 0·1295

The caloric of combustion is, according to this,

For CO $0{\cdot}557 \times 2473$ . . . . . $= 1377$ cals.

CO^2 $(0{\cdot}221 - 0{\cdot}0485) \times 8080 = 0{\cdot}1725 \times 8080 = 1394$

Total, 2771 cals.

To find the sum of caloric *necessary* for the furnace, we must calculate the caloric carried off by the gases, admitting as above that they are cooled down to the extreme limit of 200° C.

The gases are composed of—

$my = CO^2$ . . . . . $= 0{\cdot}810$

$y = CO$ . . . . . . $= 1{\cdot}300$

$N = 3{\cdot}33 \times 0{\cdot}770 \times 0{\cdot}9767$. $= 2{\cdot}504$ by formulas of § 7.

Weight of dry gases . $= 4{\cdot}614$

Water from coke . . . $= 0{\cdot}021$

Weight of moist gases . $= 4{\cdot}635$

and hence caloric carried off by gases

$$4{\cdot}635 \times 200° \times 0{\cdot}237 = 220 \text{ calories.}$$

instead of 303 of § 20.

The *necessary* amount of caloric is thus reduced by 83 calories, that is, to 3571. The blast has therefore to furnish $3571 - 2771 = 800$ calories. But the weight of blast is, according to § 7, $0{\cdot}770 \times 4{\cdot}33 \times 0{\cdot}9828 = 3{\cdot}277$, and hence for temperature of blast,

$$\frac{800}{3{\cdot}277 \times 0{\cdot}239} = \frac{800}{0{\cdot}783} = 1022°$$

And now let us calculate the caloric developed in the zone of reduction. We have,

Total caloric of combustion . . . . . 2771 cals.

Caloric developed near twyres, $0{\cdot}600 \times 2473$. 1484

Therefore caloric developed in zone of reduction 1287 cals.

Let us now bring together, in a synoptical table, the results found actually at Consett, and the results which we have found by calculation on the hypothesis that $m = 0{\cdot}623$ does not vary :—

		Actual Working.	Hypothetic Working.	Hypothetic Working.
Carbon burned at the twyres	*lbs.*	0·676	0·650	0·600
Carbon burned in the zone of reduction	"	0·113	0·1185	0·1295
Total carbon consumed, including the 0·030 taken up by the iron .	"	0·819	0·7985	0·7595
Caloric developed in zone of reduction .	*cals.*	1339	1322	1287
Caloric developed near twyres . .	"	1672	1607	1484
Total caloric of combustion .	"	3011	2929	2771
Caloric carried in by blast	"	643	657	800
Total caloric *received* or *necessary*	"	3654	3586	3571
Temperature of the gases	*deg.*	248	200	200
Temperature of blast	"	718	772	1022
Weight of blast	*lbs.*	3·751	3·562	3·277

This Table shows that after a certain limit of temperature the advantages of superheated blast become less and less, and this fact is due to several causes :—

1. The mass of air diminishes as the temperature increases.*

2. The cooling of the gases of the tunnel-head, at first very rapid, is soon limited by the development of the phenomenon of *dissociation* of CO.

3*d*, and lastly. The ratio m, which we have assumed as *constant* at and above 718°, cannot, in fact, increase above a certain maximum, for reasons already given in detail; and this limits the caloric developed in the zone of reduction.

From this it appears certain that although there is great advantage, under the conditions of the Cleveland furnaces,

* See Bell, *op. cit.*

in raising the temperature of the blast from 400° to 700°, there is not nearly the same advantage in adding 300° more, that is, heating the blast to 1000°.

It remains now to show that these conclusions would be very little modified even if the ratio m was 0·70, or even 0·80, which is the proportion at which the CO is no longer dissociated.

Let us take of the same calculations in the hypothesis of these new values of m, and let us see, in the first place, which changes would be produced on the working of No. 4 Consett furnace, if m passed from 0·623 to 0·70.

Carbon burned near the twyres . . . . . = 0·676

Oxygen furnished by the blast $\frac{4}{3} \times 0{\cdot}676 - 0{\cdot}030 = 0{\cdot}871$

Total oxide of carbon $\frac{4}{3} \times 0{\cdot}676 + 0{\cdot}403 + \frac{8}{3}(0{\cdot}0485) = 1{\cdot}443$

and hence

$$CO \text{ or } y = \frac{77 \times 1{\cdot}443}{44 \times 56 \times 0{\cdot}70} = \frac{110{\cdot}341}{83{\cdot}2} = 1^{lb}{\cdot}326 \left\{\begin{matrix}\text{with}\\ \text{carbon}\end{matrix}\right\} = 0{\cdot}568$$

$$\text{and } CO^2 \text{ or } my = 1{\cdot}326 \times 0{\cdot}70 = 0{\cdot}928 \left\{\begin{matrix}\text{with}\\ \text{carbon}\end{matrix}\right\} = 0{\cdot}253$$

Therefore total carbon of gases 0·821

Sum of carbon burned at twyres, and in limestone 0·7245

Carbon burned in zone of reduction . 0·0965

The caloric of combustion is therefore

From CO = 0·568 × 2473 . = 1405 cals.

" CO^2 = (0·253 — 0·0485) × 8080 = 1652

Total . 3057 cals.

The gases are composed of

my or CO^2 . . . . = 0·928

y or CO . . . . = 1·326

N = 3·33 × 0·871 × 0·97677 = 2·833 (formulas of § 7).

Weight of dry gases .	5·087
Water of coke . .	0·022
Weight of moist gases .	5·109

The *temperature* of these gases will not much differ from those of the actual working, as their weight is nearly the same, 5^{lb}·109 to 5^{lb}·161 (§ 20).

The caloric carried off by the gases will hence be

$$5^{lb}\cdot 109 \times 248^{\circ} \times 0\cdot 237 = 300 \text{ calories instead of } 303.$$

The *necessary* caloric will therefore be decreased by 3 calories,

which brings it to	3651 cals.
And as the caloric of combustion is . . .	3057
There remains for the heat of the blast . .	594 cals.

But the weight of the moist blast is, according to § 20, 3^{lb}·751, and hence for the temperature of the blast

$$\frac{594}{3\cdot 751 \times 0\cdot 239} = 662^{\circ} \text{ instead of } 718^{\circ},$$

that is to say, any increase in the ratio m admits of a *lowering* of the temperature of the blast, or it involves, for equal consumption of fuel, a *higher temperature of the gases.*

Let us now calculate the caloric developed in the zone of reduction:—

We have total caloric of combustion . .	3057 cals.
Caloric developed near twyres 0·675 × 2473	= 1672
And hence caloric developed in zone of reduction	1385 cals.

We can, in the same manner, calculate all the details for the case of the carbon burned near the twyres being reduced to 0·650 and 0·600. To abridge the matter, a synoptical view only is given in the following Table. It is only necessary to say that, as in the cases above given, it is assumed that the gases go off with a temperature of only 200°. We then have for the supposition that $m = 0{\cdot}70$:—

Carbon burned at the twyres	*lbs.*	0·676	0·650	0·600
Carbon burned in zone of reduction .	"	0·0965	0·1035	0·1145
Total carbon consumed, including the 0·030 absorbed by the iron	"	0·8025	0·7835	0·7445
Caloric developed in the zone of reduction	*cals.*	1385	1369	1329
Caloric developed near twyres . .	"	1672	1607	1484
Total caloric of combustion		3059	2976	2813
Caloric carried in by blast . . .	*cals.*	594	609	757
Total caloric *necessary*		3651	3583	3570
Temperature of the gases . . .	*deg.*	248	200	200
Temperature of blast	"	672	715	967
Weight of blast	*lbs.*	3·751	3·562	3·277

And now I shall, in like manner, give a synoptical table of the elements of working the Consett furnace, in the hypothesis that the ratio m could be brought to 0·80, the limit at which dissociation of CO takes place. This case is not yet know to occur in Cleveland, but it is important to have exact notions of the effects of such working.

The only uncertainty which attaches to the results is the unknown temperature of the escaping gases. For the high temperature of blast corresponding to the small consumption of 0·650 and 0·600 of carbon at the twyres, it is more than probable that the gases leave the furnace at the limit of 200°. But when the consumption is 0·676 before the twyres, it may happen that the temperature of the gases is higher than this limit, 200°, which would, of course, involve a higher temperature of blast, for from this cause alone the *necessary* caloric would be greater.

The following are the results of calculations on the double hypothesis of $m = 0{\cdot}80$, and the temperatue of gases = 200°:—

Carbon burned at the twyres . . .	*lbs.*	0·676	0·650	0·600
Carbon burned in zone of reduction .	"	0·0785	0·0865	0·0985
Total carbon, including 0·030 for combination with iron	"	0·7845	0·7665	0·7285
Caloric developed in the zone of reduction	*cals.*	1442	1428	1384
Caloric developed before twyres . .	"	1672	1607	1484
Total caloric		3114	3035	2868
Caloric carried in by blast	"	477	549	701
Total *necessary* caloric .		3591	3584	3569
Temperature of gases	*deg.*	200	200	200
Temperature of blast	"	561	645	895
Weight of blast	*lbs.*	3·751	3·562	3·277

These two last Tables confirm the conclusions drawn from the first.

For the same value of the ratio m, the carbon burned in the zone of reduction increases when, by increasing the temperature of the blast, the total consumption, as well as that near the twyres, tends to *decrease;* and yet the caloric developed in the zone of reduction is so much the less as the blast temperature is higher. If we compare the three Tables with each other, we see that to ascertain the caloric *necessary* in the furnace, the blast temperature must be so much the higher as m is less. But it is evident that, all other things being equal, it will *be more economical to get this necessary caloric by a good design of the furnace than by an overheated blast.* In any case, the *maximum of economy will be attained by the combination of high temperature of blast and a high value of the ratio* $m = \frac{CO^2}{CO}$. But this high value of m corresponds with a certain mean height of furnace, as shown in the preceding paragraphs, and presupposes that the working is slower in proportion to the greater *capacity* of the furnace—that is, from the moment a certain limit is overstepped.

And now to answer the question proposed at the commencement of this paragraph—whether there is advantage to heat the blast to 800°, 900°, or 1000°. We can boldly answer, *Yes.* For each rise in temperature of the blast there is increased economy, abstraction being made of course of the cost of maintaining and firing stoves for heating the blast. At the same time this economy decreases rapidly with the rise in temperature. The economy arising from each accession of 100° to temperature of blast is much less from 800° upwards than from 500° to 700°, and still less than between 400° and 500°, and thus *in practice it is almost useless* to exceed 700° to 800°.

§ 26. *Conclusions.*—It is now time to state the conclusions to which we have been successively led by the preceding study of the blast furnaces of Cleveland.

1. The production of blast furnaces beyond the capacity of 7000 cubic feet does not increase in proportion to that capacity (§ 1).

2. To appreciate rightly the working of blast furnaces, it is important to determine by experiment the ratio $\frac{CO^2}{CO}$ in the escaping gases. By help of this *ratio* we can not only calculate the true composition of the gases, but also the weights of blast necessary for the furnace.

3. To determine exactly the ratio $\frac{CO^2}{CO}$ it is not sufficient to draw off a certain number of samples taken from time to time *instantaneously.* The gases must be drawn off for several *hours*, and for this purpose it will be well to have recourse to an apparatus analogous to that used by Mr. Scheurer-Kestner

in his analysis of the products of combustion of coal under steam boilers (§ 9; Plate, Fig. 13).

4. Once the composition of the gases is known, if we would render an exact account of the working of the blast furnace, we must establish a balance between the caloric *received* and the caloric *expended*, and estimate separately the caloric developed in the zone of the *twyres*, and that which is produced in the zone of *reduction* (§§ 10 to 15).

5. In the application of these principles to several blast furnaces of Cleveland, we have found that the advantages of *very high* furnaces over low furnaces, result simply from the lower temperature of the upper parts of the body of the furnace. Reduction goes on more perfectly and completely by the action of CO alone, without intervention of solid carbon. We approach the *ideal* working, which supposes the solid carbon burned exclusively by the oxygen of the blast. An additional advantage, and more direct, is the less amount of sensible heat in the escaping gases (§ 21).

6. The consumption of blast furnaces depends partly on their yield. The minimum consumption corresponds to a mean speed of descent of the charges, and this varies besides with the height and absolute capacity of the furnaces (§§ 22 and 23).

7. By reason of the dissociation of the CO in the upper region of blast furnaces, the temperature of the escaping gases cannot descend below a certain limit, and *on this account* there is no advantage from the time this limit is attained in enlarging either the capacity or height of the furnaces (§ 24). A very slow rate of working and an excess of capacity are prejudicial.

8. The caloric carried in by the hot blast replaces advan-

tageously what is developed in the zone of the twyres. The relative economy due to hot blast decreases as the temperature is made higher. In practice there seems to be no real economy after the limit of 700° to 800° has been reached. The hot blast tends to raise the ratio $\frac{CO^2}{CO}$, and by cooling the upper regions of the furnace it favors *reduction without consumption of solid carbon;* that is, the *ideal* working of the apparatus.

Application of the New Method of Analysis to a French Blast Furnace.

§ 27. The investigation of which I have just summed up the principal conclusions is composed of two parts:—

I first showed how, with help of a simple apparatus, we can obtain samples, small in volume, it is true, but representing the *exact mean* composition of the escaping gases of a blast furnace, and how, by merely determining the *ratio* of $\frac{CO^2}{CO}$, we can, quite sufficiently for practice, approximate not only to the complete composition of these gases, but in a more rigorous way than by any other method, the weight of the blast consumed in the furnace.

I then showed how, with help of the elements thus determined, we can make up the *calorific balance* of blast furnaces, and thus render a complete account of all the details of its working.

By applying these principles to some English blast furnaces, and making use of the analysis made by Mr. Lowthian Bell, I endeavored to solve the important question of the *maximum height* and *limit of capacity*, and also that of the use of superheated blast.

It is quite unnecessary that I should insist on the advantages of such an analytic study of the working of blast furnaces. It is time to quit empirical methods for rational investigation.

Up to the present time the difficulties and complication of processes have stayed progress. The mode of analysis which I propose is simple, and available in every industrial laboratory. Until this mode can be applied by myself and others in France I desire to show by one example how it is possible to ascertain, even without chemical analysis, how nearly the working of a *blast* furnace approaches or falls short of the *ideal* working, that is, of *the minimum consumption possible.*

We have seen above how far the old 46 to 56 feet furnaces of Cleveland were from realizing the ideal workings; the gases escaped at a high temperature, and the proportion of carbonic acid in them is small. The ratio $\frac{CO^2}{CO}$ rarely attained 0·40. The progressive increase in the height of the furnaces overcame this double disadvantage; but it is quite evident that in cases where the gases are cool, and the ratio of CO^2 to CO approaches *unity*, the progressive increase of height is useless, and hence the great importance of determining the ratio $\frac{CO^2}{CO}$ in each particular case. We could then determine *a priori* whether there would be or not an advantage in modifying the dimensions of the furnaces. By these studies abortive trials, such as are alluded to in § 2, may be avoided—blast furnaces raised to great heights, and then decapitated and reduced to the old dimensions.

We have in France numerous coke blast furnaces of ordinary dimensions, the consumption in which is not greater than in the great furnaces of Cleveland, and yet the ores there treated are neither richer nor more fusible than those of the north of England. These furnaces would gain very little in being increased in height, for the gases are now relatively cool and the consumption small, so that *a priori* we may feel sure that the ratio $\frac{CO^2}{CO}$ is not far from unity.

Let us show by an example that even without an analysis, properly so called, it is possible to arrive at an approximate determination of this ratio, and to ascertain up to a certain point if it be possible to improve the working of the furnace. It is, however, quite clear that in any case it would be most useful to be able to confirm these approximations by a direct examination of the gases of the tunnel-head.

I take as an example one of the blast furnaces of Pouzin, of the *Société de l'Horme*, situated on the borders of the Rhône, between Valence and Montélimart. The data have reference to 1857—somewhat old, but the ores, the coke, the consumption, etc., are even now the same. The yield alone is different. In 1857 the yield was only 18 tons; it is now 25 to 30 tons.

The section of the furnace is tapering (fig. 12). The height is 55 feet, and the capacity 4000 cubic feet. The blast was heated to 290°, and supplied at pleasure by two or three twyres. The temperature of the gases escaping was 150°.

The normal yield was forge pig No. 4. The ore is the red hæmatite of the Oxford formation, with an argilo-calcareous matrix. Its average composition is represented by the following:—

Peroxide of iron . .	60, with 42 of iron.
Clay	21
Carbonate of lime . .	15
Water	4
	100

The various elements of the working of the furnace are put together in the following Table, giving the *balance* of raw materials and yield. This is the model of such tables used by me for a long time for my lectures at the École des Mines.

BALANCE OF RAW MATERIAL AND OF YIELD of one of the Blast Furnaces of Pouzin (1857), the pig-iron containing 3 per cent. of carbon, 2 per cent. silicium, 1 per cent. of other foreign matters.

Raw materials per lb. of pig yielded.	Distribution of the materials.	Yield.		
		Pig-iron.	Slag.	Gas.
lbs.				
Ore . . . 2·340				
Composed of—	*lbs.*			
(0·60) Fe^2O^3 1·404	Peroxide of iron, 1·343 { Fe .	0·940	..	..
	{ O .	..	0·055	0·403
	Peroxide of iron, 0·061 { FeO	..		..
	1·404 { O .	..		0·006
(0·21) clay. 0·491	0·060 { Silica and earth reduced { Si, etc.	0·030	..	..
	{ O .	..	..	0·030
	See § 7.			
	0.431 undecomposed clay. .	..	0·431	..
(0·15) carbonate of lime 0·351	Lime	..	0·196	..
	CO^2	..	..	0·155
(0·04) water, 0·094	Steam	..	..	0·094
2·340				
Flux . . . 0·600	Lime	..	0·326	..
	CO^2	..	..	0·264
Coke . . . 1·200	Carbon . . . . . . *lbs.* 0·970	0·030	..	0·940
	Cinder . . . . . . " 0·180	..	0·180	..
	Water . . . . . . " 0·050	..	..	0·050
	Coke . . . " 1·200			
Total of solid raw material 4·146	Giving	1·000	1·198	1·942

NOTE.—To have the total weight of the gases, we must add to 1·942 the weight of blast supplied. We shall see that this may be valued approximately at 4·875. It is also to be remarked in passing, that when we know the composition of the matrix of the ores, and *of the ashes of the coke*, we can also, by means of this table, determine *a priori* the composition of the slags.

In order now to appreciate, by this Table, the real working of the furnace, we must first make an approximate estimate of the caloric *consumed.*

This is composed (by § 10) of four parts, of which two can be determined with sufficient exactness, and the two others only approximately.

The first part includes, on the one hand, the caloric absorbed by the *reduction*, which scarcely varies with the nature of the ores if they be peroxide; and, on the other hand, the caloric possessed by the iron in flowing from the furnace.

The caloric of *reduction* is . . .	1984 cals.	(§ 11).
For caloric of fusion for forge iron, No. 4, say	310	
Total . .	2294 cals.	

In the second part, there is first the caloric in the slags. As the ore is fusible, we may put this at 500 calories per lb. of slags, instead of 550, which gives for 1·198 lb. of slag, 599 calories.

We have then the caloric taken for decomposition of the limestone, the vaporization of water, and the decomposition of the moisture of the air. It is only this last element which is uncertain, because we do not know the exact weight of the blast. But we may admit, provisionally, as the weight, 4·50 lb., considering what we know of the carbon consumed and the results derived from the Cleveland furnaces.

The third part is the caloric carried off by the gases. We know their temperature. As to their weight, it is sufficient to add to the gases from the charges the air of the blast, that is, according to our table, $4{\cdot}5 + 1{\cdot}942 = 6{\cdot}442$; and the fourth part is the caloric lost by radiation, etc., from the walls of the furnace; and we may admit 300 calories, judging by Mr. Bell's data for Cleveland.

Starting from these principles, we shall find for the caloric consumed by the Pouzin furnaces as follows:—

1. Caloric of reduction and of fusion of pig-iron = 2294 cals.

2. Caloric in the slag, 1·198 × 500 . . . = 599 "
   Caloric absorbed by the limestone, of ore and flux, 0·991 × 373·5 . . . . = 355 "
   Caloric absorbed for evaporation of water of ore, and coke, 0·144 × 606 . . . = 87 "
   Caloric taken for decomposition of moisture of air, 0·0062 × 4·5 × 3222 . . . = 90 "

3. Caloric carried off by gases, 6·442 × 150° × 0·237 . . . . = 229 "

4. Caloric lost by radiation, etc. . . . . = 300 "

Total caloric *consumed* or *necessary* . 3954 cals.

This figure must also represent the caloric *received*, which is made up of the caloric of combustion, and the caloric carried in by the blast.

Now, admitting that the weight of blast is 4lb ·50, we have, as approximate value of the caloric carried in by blast (§ 16),

$$4{\cdot}50 \times 290^\circ \times 0{\cdot}239 = 312 \text{ calories.}$$

There remains, therefore, for the caloric of combustion, 3642 calories, whilst the total calorific power of the carbon is 0·940 × 8080 = 7595 calories; so that we have, as final result, the caloric developed in the furnace $\frac{3642}{7595} = 0{\cdot}48$ of the calorific power of the carbon burned. This is precisely the proportion found for the large blast furnace of Clarence Works (§ 17), which seems to prove already that the Pouzin furnace, notwithstanding its small capacity, was working under good conditions.

But as we know the carbon burned and the caloric developed, it is easy to find, by the help of two equations, the value of my or CO^2 and y or CO.

We have, on one hand, the equation (1.) of § 7:

$$\frac{3}{7}y + \frac{3}{11}my = p,$$

and, on the other hand, we know that the caloric of combustion is due to carbon burned to CO and CO^2. The formula (4.) of § 15 gives for this caloric

$$\frac{3}{7}y \times 2473 + \left(\frac{3}{11}my - b\right)8080 = 3642,$$

a formula which may be written thus:

$$(4.)\ \left(\frac{3}{7} \times 2473 + \frac{3}{11}m \times 8080\right)y = 3642 + 8080 \times b = Q.$$

And from these two equations (1.) and (4.) we have

$$m = \frac{11}{7}\left(\frac{Q - 2473.p}{8080\,p - Q}\right);\ y = \frac{7}{3}\left(\frac{8080.p - Q}{5607}\right)$$

hence $$my = \frac{11}{3}\left(\frac{Q - 2473.p}{5607}\right)$$

Let us now apply these expressions to the data of the furnace of Pouzin.

b is the carbon contained in the limestone $0^{lb}\cdot951 = 0\cdot600 + \cdot351$, therefore $= b\ 0\cdot12 \times 0\cdot951 = 0\cdot114$;

p is the carbon consumed, plus the carbon supplied by the limestone;

therefore $p = 0\cdot940 + 0\cdot114 = 1\cdot054$,

hence $Q = 3642 + 8080 \times 0\cdot114 = 4563$ calories,

$$m = \frac{11}{7}\left(\frac{4563 - 2606}{8516 - 4563}\right) = \frac{11}{7}\left(\frac{1957}{3953}\right) = \frac{21527}{27671} = 0\cdot78,$$

$$y = 1^{lb}\cdot645 \text{ and } my = 1^{lb}\cdot280.$$

The gases therefore contain:

1·645 CO,	containing	0^{lb}·705	carbon
1·280 CO^2	"	0 ·349	"
	Total carbon	1^{lb}·054 $= p$.	

And from the values of m and of y we can deduce the quantities of oxygen and nitrogen which must be supplied by the blast, using the formulas of § 7.

The formula (3.) determines the oxygen given up by the charge to the gases:

$$d = \frac{8}{3} \times 0{\cdot}114 + 0{\cdot}423 = 0^{lb}{\cdot}727$$

and formula (2.) gives for total oxygen of blast

$$x = \frac{y}{77}(44 + 56 \times m) - 0{\cdot}727 = 1^{lb}{\cdot}146$$

and hence for oxygen of dry air,

z 0·97677 x	$= 1^{lb}$·119
For nitrogen, 3·33 z	$=$ 3 ·726
That is, for dry air	$=$ 4 ·845
Moisture of air, 0·0062 × 4·845 .	$=$ 0 ·030
Weight of moist air	$=$ 4 ·875

And finally the gas will be composed of

CO^2	1^{lb}·280
CO	1 ·645
N	3 ·726
Dry gases . . .	6 ·651
Water of charges . .	0 ·144
Moist gases . . .	6 ·795

We see now that the weight of air in blast, and of the escaping gases, are somewhat greater than the weights we assumed *a priori*. But in reference to calorific effects, there is very nearly compensation; the excess of blast, 0·375, would *take in* 25 calories more into the furnace, whilst the excess of gases would *carry off* 14 to 15 calories above the numbers deduced by calculation.

There would therefore be in reality an excess of caloric carried in of 10 to 11 calories, which should be compensated by a less caloric of combustion; that is, the caloric of combustion would be reduced from 3642 to 3632. If we would go very accurately to work, we must begin the calculation again with this last number in order to determine the values of *m* and *y*. The number Q, in the preceding formulas, would be reduced by 10 units. We should have 4553 calories, instead of 4563. But it is quite evident that this correction would be insignificant. It would give the value of CO 0^{lb}·004 more (1·649 instead of 1·645), and the ratio *m* would scarcely be affected. In short, the figures above given represent sufficiently near, for practical purposes, the real state of things; and the result is, that the working of the Pouzin furnace is very satisfactory.

The ratio *m* has almost attained the limit 0·80, at which the dissociation of CO does not take place. The gases are rich in CO^2 and yet cool. In these circumstances an increase of the height of the furnace could produce no sensible useful effect (§ 24).

The consumption could not be reduced below 0·970 of pure carbon, unless the blast were superheated, as at Consett. This advantageous working of the Pouzin furnace must, in my opinion, be attributed, in great measure, to the high tapering form of action. The gases are very uniformly distributed, and the reduction goes on very regularly. At one time, the director of the works tried to enlarge the tunnel-head without modifying the system of charging. There resulted *immediately* a less regular working, and a greater consumption. Since that time the yield has been increased by forcing the weight of blast, but the consumption has not sunk below 0·970 of pure carbon.

We now see, that indirectly, even without determining by experimenting the value of $m = \frac{CO^2}{CO}$ we can come at an approximate estimate of the manner in which the carbon is consumed in blast furnaces, and thus appreciate the relative economy of their working. But this *indirect* determination of the value of $\frac{CO^2}{CO}$ depends on an estimate more or less hypothetic of the caloric consumed. It will always be preferable to determine the ratio by an analysis of the gases, which allows of our calculating with perfect exactness the caloric *received.*

This is a system of controlling the working of blast furnaces easily realized. It may be confidently recommended to iron-masters. They can thus ascertain in what respect their apparatus is faulty, and remedy the fault with confidence.

§ 28. *Another example of French blast furnaces.*—I have now shown by the example of Pouzin, that it is not always necessary to have great *height* of blast furnace to get satisfactory results. I might multiply examples. I shall take the blast furnaces of *Denain* of 1865, in which, with a volume of 2750 cubic feet, and a height of 42 feet only, they have arrived at a yield of 30 tons per day of forge iron, consuming only 1·150 to 1·200 tons of coke of 15 % ashes per ton of pig, and this with argillaceous ores yielding only 32 % to 35 %. These favorable results are realized chiefly by a more rational system of charging, and also, as at Pouzin, by their having a more *contracted region of fusion* than most of the English blast furnaces.

Take now, as example, No. 1 furnace of Montluçon, St. Jacques' Works, of which in 1867 the principal elements were,

Capacity	4250 c. ft.
Height	49 feet.
Temperature of the blast .	315°

Temperature of escaping gases, 100°, arising from the hydrated state of the ores.

Yield in twenty-four hours, 24 tons of gray forge iron.

Charges—hydrated ore in grains, with $\frac{1}{10}$ slag from forge, contains about 40 % as a mean.

Consumption per lb. of iron,

"	"	coke	1·145 at 17 % of ash and 3 % of water, or 0·916 pure carbon.
"	"	ores	2·547
"	"	flux	0·906
Slag produced . .			1·470

This is again an example of economical working, and if we apply to this the methods of calculation above given in detail for Pouzin, we should again find a high value for the ratio $\frac{CO^2}{CO}$. An increase in height would certainly not diminish the consumption, already very low.

9

The *only possible* economy is that which would result from the use of higher temperature of blast.

If now I am asked whence arises this great difference between the working of the French furnaces here named and those of the older types of Cleveland, I can only suggest the following reasons:—

1. The section of the French furnaces is generally more tapering than that of English furnaces. Hence there is a better distribution of the gases; the reduction goes on in the upper regions with a less combustion of solid carbon. It has been already remarked that it is to this difference in section, *in shape*, that part of the economy of the furnace of Clarence 1866, compared to Ormesby 1867, and Clarence 1853, is to be attributed.

2. The *manner of charging* is more studied in France. Its influence on the distribution of the blast is well known. It is seen that thus they approach most nearly to the *ideal* working, that is, to the *reduction* of the ores without burning solid carbon.

3. Lastly, the region of fusion near the twyres, *the hearth*, appears to me to be generally *too wide* in England. In the smallest furnaces of Cleveland the diameter of the hearth is never less than 6 feet, and in most of those of 10,000 cubic feet and 17,000 cubic capacity, it reaches 7 feet 3 inches to 8 feet 3 inches, and even 9 feet, and yet the height is often *less* than this diameter. But the capacity of the region of fusion has a direct influence on the consumption. For fusing a refractory ore, it is not necessary alone to have a certain amount of caloric, the caloric must be well *distributed*, so that the local temperature shall be intense, which cannot be realized save in a contracted space.

We know by Tunner's experiments on the temperatures of the region of fusion, that near each twyre the zone of combustion is always very limited, and that if we desire to have a *high mean temperature* the zone of fusion must be contracted. Whatever be the dimensions of the body of a blast furnace this high temperature cannot be realized with a relatively low consumption, except by the use of narrow hearths high relatively to their diameter. This is a precaution too often neglected, not only in blast furnaces but also in lead and copper furnaces and in cupola furnaces.

Additional Note.

During the impression of these pages, I have engaged in certain experiments on the caloric of the iron and slags running from the blast furnace. I shall publish these results soon. In the mean time I must say that the numbers adopted by Mr. Bell now appear to me somewhat high, and that in the estimates above given there may be some correction to make.

All the general conclusions to which my study of the blast furnace has led me are in no way affected by this—only, the caloric carried off by *radiation from the walls of the furnace should be about* 100 *calories more than above given.*

APPENDIX.

APPENDIX.

Note I. p. 42.

On this subject Dr. Percy has the following observations: "In all the preceding experimental investigations concerning the composition of the gaseous currents of blast furnaces there is one source of error which should be particularly borne in mind. The gas from any given furnace was collected at successive intervals, and it is doubtful whether any method could have been adapted for collecting it simultaneously at different depths, except by the insertion of tubes through the sides of the furnace, which would have involved much additional expense, and which might not, after all, have yielded perfectly satisfactory results, as the gas from the centre, owing to variations in the velocity of the gaseous current in different parts of the same transverse sectional area, may not have the same composition as near the sides. Now, identity of conditions cannot be measured, even in the same furnace, for an hour, much less for a day; so that the gas collected at intervals, however short, from exactly the same part of the furnace, working with the same charge, may not have the same composition."*

In Dr. Wedding's translation of Percy's work, the remark is intercalated: "The most accurate average composition of

* Percy, vol. ii. p. 443.

the gases will be got by analysis of the gases drawn from the main tube leading off the gases from the tunnel-head for further use. Here they are thoroughly mixed."

NOTE II. pp. 50, 52.

On the subject of refractory ores—" *Minerais Refractaires*" —" *Strengflüssige Erze*" as opposed to " *Leichtflüssige Erze*"— Mr. Lowthian Bell makes the following remark in section xliii. of his *Chemical Phenomena of Iron Smelting:* " In connection with the greater or less consumption of fuel, German writers on Iron-smelting make use of the terms 'Strengflüssig' and 'Leichtflüssig.' If these words have to be taken in their literal sense of comparative susceptibility to fusion, their use, in my opinion, may lead to error. There are, no doubt, some differences in the melting points of different kinds of iron and slag, but these, I apprehend, are trifling, and cannot account for the marked alterations just spoken of in the quantity of fuel required for mere liquefaction. The actual cause of the lesser quantity of consumption of fuel in small furnaces I have conceived and described as being due to difference in susceptibility of *reduction*, and not fusion.

There is however a considerable difference in the temperature required for the *complete formation* of different slags. According to Plattner's experiments, although the temperature of fusion of the slag itself *when formed* varies much less for different proportions of acid and bases, forming singulo-silicates, bisilicates, and trisilicates, the temperature at which *slags are formed* varies considerably. In general, singulo-silicates require a higher temperature for formation—are

"Strengflüssiger" or "Strengschmelziger"—than bisilicates: and of *singulo-silicates*,

that of Alumina takes for formation	. .	2400° C.
Magnesia	. . .	2200° to 2250° "
Barytes	. . . .	2100° to 2200° "
Lime	. . . .	2100° to 2150° "
Iron and manganese	.	1789° to 1832° "

The silicates of oxides of manganese and iron (protoxide) differ very little from each other.

The bi- and trisilicates of the different earths are formed at a lower temperature.

Of the bisilicates	those of	barytes and lime form at	2100°
"	"	barytes and alumina	2050°
"	"	lime and magnesia	2000°
"	"	lime and alumina	1918° to 1950°

The temperature required for the formation of compound silicate (for instance, $CaO^3\ Si^2O^3 + AlO^3\ Si^2O^3$, a frequently occuring slag) from the earths composing them, is very much higher than that at which slags which have been already fused can be melted. As the slags coming from smelting processes are seldom formed by fusing together these independent components, but more frequently from a mixture of silicates already formed—partly from the ores, etc., and generally of manifold combinations of the oxides of the earths—the temperature required for the formation of the new slag or compounded silicates will lie between their point of fusion and the temperature which would be necessary to form this new slag from the separate simple substances.

Refractory slags—"strengflüssige"—which are always indications of faulty working of the furnace, arise either from insufficient temperature, or from injudicious combination of the charges, as when too much silica and too little of the bases, or the contrary, exists, or if among the bases there be an excess of alumina and magnesia. Such slags are recognized by their *pasty* nature, their earthy, half-fused appearance, and by the air-holes pervading them. On the other hand, the *charge* is a good combination when the slags flow out of a good consistency—as free from metal as possible—and when, for a given consumption of fuel, the maximum of ores can be used.

Dr. Percy, while objecting to the principle of Plattner's method—because it assumes that alloys of gold, silver, and platina fuse at the mean temperature of the component parts —says we may accept his results as affording practical information of value. "The melting points of metals and their alloys are fixed and unvarying, except under extraordinary conditions of great pressure, and as they extend through a very wide range of temperature they may be conveniently employed in the determination and comparison of high temperature."*

Plattner himself considered that he had only determined temperatures correctly *proportioned* to each other, and not *absolute* thermometric limits.

This note is to explain what is meant by "Strengflüssige Erzen"—"minerais refractaire"—as used by continental writers.

Note III. p. 87.

The beautiful inductive investigation of the large yield of pig-iron with small consumption of fuel in the Styrian and

* Percy, *op. cit.* vol. i. p. 48.

Carinthian furnaces, in section xliii. of Mr. Bell's work, is well worthy of study in reference to this conclusion of M. Ebelmen.

Also Dr. Percy, vol. ii. p. 446, quotes Ebelmen in detail as follows: "If we compare two kinds of fuel, which act with different rapidity upon the air and carbonic acid, such as coke and charcoal, it is very plain that it will be necessary to increase the mass of the least combustible of the two, relatively to that of the ore, in order that oxidation of the iron should not take place to a greater extent in one case than in another. Thus experience has proved that, on the average, twice as much coke (by weight) is required as charcoal to produce in the blast furnace pig-iron of the same amount and of the same quality. In the same manner may be explained the difference of consumption of the same furnace, working always with the same fuel, according as it is desired to produce different qualities of pig-iron. Thus, much more charcoal is consumed in order to obtain gray pig-iron than white." Dr. Percy remarks—"There is no doubt about this fact, though there may be much as to Ebelmen's explanation of it." Dr. Percy's remark I do not agree with. The "fact" *is open to the greatest doubt.*

NOTE IV. p. 87.

The fact that charcoal decomposes CO^2 (burns under a current of CO^2 giving off CO) more rapidly than hard or soft coke, is proved incontestably by Mr. Bell's experiments, Nos. 818 and 819, p. 75, No. I. Part II. of Journal of Iron and Steel Institute.

Note V.

It is proposed in this Note to give a brief history of the "Theory of the Blast Furnace," with the view of showing how very recently correct notions on the subject were first published, even of the chemical phenomena involved; and that it is not more than ten years since any concentrated attention was given to investigate the physical phenomena, that is, the calorific phenomena accompanying the chemical phenomena, by a knowledge of which alone the *natural limit to the economy of fuel* can be determined. And further it is proposed to examine whether any tenable objections have been made to Mr. Bell's theory of this subject, now reproduced and perhaps rendered even more precise by Mr. Gruner in the text, §§ 4 and 5, where he defines what is, in *respect of consumption of fuel*, the *ideally perfect working* of a blast furnace.

As to the theory of the blast furnace.

In 1837–1838, Lampadius* taught his pupils that we may divide the blast furnace into four zones from above downwards, viz., into zones of calcination, reduction, smelting, and collection of products, and that therefore the charges in moving downwards must undergo the following changes. In the zone of calcination, the gaseous substances are driven off, the water, and in some part the carbonic acid of the ores

* Wilhelm August Lampadius, b. 1772, d. 1842, was chosen by the celebrated Werner, founder of the Royal School of Mines, to be Professor of Chemistry and Metallurgy at Freyberg. He introduced Lavoisier's Chemistry at Freyberg. He published his *Handbuch der Allgemeinen Hüttenkunde* in 1801–1810, 4 vols., and was all his life active in the publication of important works on metallurgy and chemistry.

and fluxes. In the reducing zone, extending downwards nearly to the boshes, the desoxidation of the oxides of iron, by the carbonic oxide generated near the twyres, goes on, and the rest of the CO^2 is expelled. A small portion of carburetted hydrogen also comes into play, and there is also reduction by contact with incandescent solid carbon. Towards the end of reduction the reduced iron sinters together with the substances forming the slags. The other substances present in the charges, as manganese, phosphorus, sulphuric acid, titanic acid, and such like, are only very partially desoxidized in this zone. In the zone of smelting, extending down to a point in the hearth above the twyres, the reduction of the ore is completed, and also a part of the manganese, and the acids and earths desoxidized. There are therefore formed compounds of manganese, phosphorus, sulphur, silicium, aluminium with iron, and these mix or combine with the iron, which here also takes up a certain proportion of *carbon*, and thus *Roh eisen*, cast-iron, pig-iron, *fonte*, is produced, a substance more fusible than malleable iron. In February, 1839, Lampadius published this statement of his views in a small work, *Die Neuere Fortschritte im Gebiete der Gesammten Hüttenkunde*, *i. e.* "Latest Progress in Metallurgical Science and Practice." That this was not the generally received theory of the process going on in the blast furnace is shown by the following abstract of a paper "On the Reduction of Iron Ores in the Blast Furnace by Hot and Cold Blast, and with Raw and Coked Fuel," published by Karsten in 1839.*

It has been asserted, says Karsten, that in cases where not

* *Archiv für Mineralogie*, etc., vol. xii. p. 528.

only fusion has to be effected, but reduction of oxides must take place, this reduction is hastened by complete contact of the fuel with the ores; and hence it has been recommended that the fuel and ore should be mixed before being charged into the furnace. But it is well known, that it is only necessary to *begin* reduction on the surface of a body, and that the process penetrates to the interior without any immediate contact with the reducing agent being necessary. M. Le Play has, it is true, recently and repeatedly called attention to the reducing power of carbonic oxide. He has shown that oxides of iron, in circumstances where they could not come in contact with solid carbon, were reduced at a certain temperature by carbonic oxide made in a tube in which carbon was at one end, oxide of iron at the other, and the air was sealed up with the two—that the carbonic oxide first formed was transformed to carbonic acid by the oxygen of the ore, and reconverted to carbonic oxide by the carbon, and so on in succession, till either the carbon was burned or the ore was completely reduced. "But," says Karsten, "the oxides of iron are unquestionably *not* reduced in this way in the blast furnace, because the CO formed by the incandescent carbon in contact with CO^2 rushes too rapidly past to the top of the furnace, and because the oxides of iron are everywhere in contact with incandescent carbon, by which the reduction can be begun without its being necessary to decompose a gas, which would, besides, have to take place under circumstances which would rather favor the *generation* than the decomposition of the gas (CO^2)."

Assuming that the process of reduction above described was correctly conceived, Karsten proceeds to take into consideration the products of combustion, and concludes, "that the formation of carbonic oxide takes place in the upper part of the furnace by the reduction of the ores by solid carbon." "But," says he, "the reduction when only CO is formed takes *twice as much fuel* as when CO^2 is formed; and if there were any means of preventing the formation of CO here, this would be at the same time the means of reducing the ores with the least expenditure of fuel."

We now know that the air blown into the furnace at the twyres is almost instantaneously transformed into carbonic oxide, and this gas, in its passage up the body of the furnace, acts more or less directly in reducing ores; that is, *with* or without the aid of the solid carbon (see *ante*, p. 25). We also know that, in the presence of CO^2, iron is practically re-oxidized, and that in the presence of equal volumes of CO and CO^2, peroxide and metallic iron are both brought to the state of oxide.

The doctrine of Lampadius was much nearer the truth than that of Karsten, and is, in fact, the *explanation* still given of what goes on in the blast furnace (see Percy, vol. ii. p. 444), but great strides had yet to be made, and that very year, 1839, before the printing of the number of Karsten's *Archiv* in which his notions above given was finished, Bunsen's first experiments on the composition of the gases at different depths of the blast furnace, at Veckerhagen, were published as an Appendix to Karsten's paper. In his report of the experiments Bunsen writes: "They prove that too much weight has hitherto been laid on the desoxidation of CO^2 to CO at the cost of incandescent carbon. Some of my experiments demonstrate that, in the combustion of charcoal, the first immediate product is CO, provided there be no surplus supply of oxygen to burn the CO to CO^2, and thus one-half the calorific effect of the fuel is lost."

Thus began to be formed a theory of the blast furnace. But such as it was, the theory was still only a *qualitative* analysis, so to speak. Bunsen first began the *quantitative* analysis, and first gave a *calculation of the quantity of caloric used in the furnace*, and of the *quantity carried off in the gases*, and pointed out for what purposes this lost heat might be made available. For a particular case of analysis of the gases collected 5 feet under the tunnel-head, 49·55 per cent., or *one-half of the fuel* was proved to go off as CO, and was lost, and that besides the sensible heat of the gases themselves being 993° C., 25 % more of the fuel was lost in this way; so that 75 % altogether was lost.*

The researches of Ebelmen on the composition of the blast furnace gases were begun at the same time as Bunsen's researches, but were published a year or two later.† Ebelmen made his calculations of the quantities of caloric used, and of the temperature in the furnace, by adopting Dulong's calorimetric results, given in the *Comptes Rendus*, 1838, p. 874,‡ and arrived at the conclusion that 64·8 % of the fuel went off in the gases and was lost. Ebelmen pointed out that the gases escaping would suffice for heating the blast, supplying the steam for blast engine, and for the desiccation of the wood used in the furnace itself.

* Karsten's *Archiv*, vol. xii. p. 547; 1839.

† *Annales des Mines*, 1841–43, and collected Memoirs, published in Paris, 1861.

‡ For the combustion of

C to CO^2 Dulong found 7167 cals., but it is 8080

CO to CO^2 " " 2634 cals., " " 2473.

Such was the progress made towards a rational theory of the blast furnace—chemical and physical—and of its application to determining the calorific efficiency of the fuel consumed, in 1842; and very little progress was made for several years afterwards either in diffusing or extending the notions then attained to.

And now it is interesting to show how, in this department as in many others, *art is the mother of science.*

Long before an analysis of the gases of blast furnaces was made, or could have been made, practical men perceived the uses to which the gases could be turned. For this object a quotation from Dr. Percy's great work, vol. ii. p. 663, will suffice: "In June, 1814, Berthier published an interesting and important paper* on the successful application, in France, of the waste gas to various purposes, such as the conversion of iron into steel by cementation, and the burning of lime and bricks. The credit of this application is due to M. Aubertot, who was a proprietor of ironworks in the department of Cher. He obtained a patent for it in France in 1811. Berthier visited four works, either belonging to, or managed by, M. Aubertot, so that his description was founded on personal observation; and it is very just to his memory to state, that he seems clearly to have foreseen the value of the application in question. The calorific effect of the waste gases was rightly attributed by Berthier, partly to the sensible heat, and partly to the heat developed by combustion in contact with atmospheric air."

Mr. Moses Teague took a patent on this matter in 1832. Mr. James Palmer Budd obtained a patent for the applica-

* *Journal des Mines*, 35, p. 375; June, 1814.

tion of the "heat, flames, and gases of the blast furnace to the heating of hot-blast stoves" in 1840. This application was carried into practice at Ystelyfera, and so satisfied was Mr. Budd with the success that he even ventured to draw the following conclusion: "It would appear to be more profitable to employ a blast furnace, if as a gas generator only, even if you smelted nothing in it, and carried off its heated vapors (*sic*) by flues to your boilers and stoves, than to employ a separate fire to each boiler and each stove. These considerations irresistibly suggest to me a great revolution in metallurgical practice, a new arrangement, in fact, of furnaces and works by which considerably above £1,000,000 a year might be saved in the iron trade alone (1848)." This was excusable in the first enthusiasm, but it is well known that it is only when a low class of coal has to be used that *generator* or "producer" gases are not wasteful, except where *intensity* of heat is required.

Let us revert now to the progress made since 1842 in the chemical and physical theory of the blast furnace. Bunsen's calculations were founded on the truth of "*Welter's law*," by which the caloric evolved in the furnace would be to the potential caloric of the gases escaping as the weight of the oxygen burned in the furnace is to that of the oxygen required for complete combustion of the gases escaping. Welter's law is not universally true, and it is certainly not true for this application.

Ebelmen could only refer to the *calorimetric* determinations of Dulong for his calculation of the development of caloric in the combustion of carbon and carbonic oxide.* Since then

* It is interesting to mention here that in the *Handbuch der Chemie* of L. Gmelin, published in 1843, he remarks—"Dulong's determination of the

we have the more accurate determinations of MM. Favre and Silbermann, and of Professor Andrews, of this and other essential elements of the calculations in question, and besides these, more accurate knowledge of specific heats of all substances, as may be gathered from the study of modern works on chemistry and physics; or, for the present special question, in the works of Dr. Percy, Mr. Bell, M. Gruner, and Mr. Schinz.

In 1863–64 the "Metallurgy of Iron and Steel" was published by Dr. Percy, and this was certainly an epoch in the literature of this important subject, not only in England, where it was the first work on metallurgy of any scientific value ever published, but in Germany and in France, where the work was immediately translated by eminently qualified metallurgists. The German translation by Dr. Wedding is still in progress.

Dr. Percy says, p. 444, vol. ii.—"As far as I am able to judge, the importance, whether in a scientific or practical point of view, of the results of the analysis of the blast furnace gases has been somewhat over-estimated. Temperature, carbonic oxide, and incandescent carbon, *explain* all the phenomena of the blast furnace," and Dr. Percy does perfectly explain them in the next subsequent pages of his book, with just a little more preciseness than Lampadius did in 1838.

quantity of caloric from the combustion of carbonic oxide is, *without doubt, much too high. If* it were correct, then carbon in combining with the *first atom* of oxygen must develop *much less* caloric than with the second, which *is extremely improbable.*" But we know now that this is exactly what occurs—so the exact science of to-day was a stumbling-block to the ablest men of science only twenty years ago. Let us learn to be cautious in accepting even scientific authority as final, and very humble in the assertion of scientific opinions.

The physical phenomena—the *calorific phenomena* of the blast furnace were not, as far as my knowledge of the subject goes, taken into serious consideration till Mr. Schinz, of Strasburg, began his investigations about 1864. In 1868 the *Dokumente betreffend den Hohofen zur Darstellung von Roheisen* was published,* and in this, for the first time, the advancement in calorimetric determinations of the heat *absorbed* or *evolved* in chemical combinations, which science had gained since the early experiments of Dulong, Despretz, and others, were applied to determine the *principles* on which the *economy* of the blast furnace depends. Schinz's work contains much useful information. Laborious calculations are unfortunately expended on questions of no practical interest, and some fundamental mistakes were made in this first attempt to construct a balance-sheet between caloric received and caloric expended altogether vitiating the results. The original, or, better, the translation, should nevertheless be in the hands of every student of the phenomena of the blast furnace, if only to show the difficulties and complications of the question, and how even men of unquestionable scientific attainment may be misled by one false step in their reasoning into a maze of calculations based often on guess-work and having no practical use.

Schinz undertook a series of experiments on the conditions under which ores *are reduced*, and the laws upon which this reduction is based, upon which he "spent years of labor in

* A good translation of this work by W. H. Maw and M. Müller, under the title *Researches on the Action of the Blast Furnace*, was published in 1870.

order to acquire this knowledge as exactly as possible."* These investigations aspired to determine for the process of reduction,

a. The influence of temperature.

b. The influence of the quantity of gas passing in unit of time.

c. The influence of the proportion of CO in the gases.

d. The influence of time of exposure to gases.

e. The influence of the nature of the ores; and

f. The conditions of carburation of the iron.

Schinz after a time convinced himself that correct and useful results could only be attained if such gases were experimented with as are really to be found in the blast furnace.

These gases he prepared artificially, so far as the proportion of CO to nitrogen is concerned.

The pyrometer used was a thermo-electric element, very specially arranged, and for which Schinz calculated tables of correction, but the relative thermometric determinations he considered as generally too high.

Ten different qualities of ores were experimented upon: Red Hæmatite—brown ores from Hayange—from Nassau—Spathic ores from Siegen—Oolithic ores from Namur— artificial ores—viz., 100 oxide of iron, 100 carbonate of lime, 25 carbon, and others as bases of pure oxide of iron.

The experiments made with the "Reductometer" impressed him with the opinion that there is no justification for a distinction between the zone of fusion and that of carburation;

* *Dokumente*, p. 57; translation, p. 88. *Op. cit.* p. 1; translation, p. 6 *et seq.*

for the carburation begins at a low temperature with the appearance of the first molecules of metallic iron. This temperature he found by his pyrometer to be between 780° and 786° C. And further on in his reasearches Schinz writes—"It is therefore almost impossible that the iron can receive carbon from any other source than the carbonic oxide, or at other place than in the zone of reduction."

The experiments showed that at 400° *of the thermo-electric pyrometer* no reduction takes place. Measured otherwise, Mr. L. Bell found that *reduction is complete under* this temperature (see *postea*, p. 152).

a. We must cite an example of the influence of temperature* on the rate of reduction of red iron ore from Dillenburg, sp. gr. 5·4—30 % of oxygen combined.

No. of Experiment.	Hourly absorption of O.	Temperatures (by pyrom.)
21	1·60	421°
22	2·55	546° to 621°
23	2·70	823° to 861°
24	4·45	884°

b. The influence of quantity of gases passing in unit of time was proved to be such that, for instance, with a double flow of gas, the reduction was as 5·62 % to 4·75 % of the total oxygen absorbed per hour, for temperatures varying from 499° upwards in the one case to 720° upwards in the case of the less supply of gas.†

c. The influence of the quantity of CO in the gases was found to be such that when 49·32 % CO was present, the reduction per hour was just *twice as much* as when the

* *Op. cit.* p. 77; trans. 112.

† Consult Bell's work, section iv. and section xi.

contents were only 34·65 per cent. for the same temperature and same *absolute quantity* of gas.

d. The influence of time was, as might be expected, quite evident through all the experiments.

e. The quality of the ore. The result of these experiments was that "the richest and most compact ores gave under all circumstances the *most favorable coefficient of reduction*, but neither the specific gravity nor the contents of iron in the ores have any recognized proportion to the reduction, so that experiments for each ore would have to be made.

f. The carburation of the iron. The experiments prove that carburation of the iron begins with its reduction, that is, as soon as metallic iron appears. The observation that the carbon of the CO *combines with the iron instead of reducing it* is proved by experiment 50; for instance, where an abundant carburation took place at 780° (by pyrometer), although not one-half of the iron was reduced from the peroxide. The greater the percentage of carbonic oxide in the gases the greater is the transfer of carbon to the iron when reduction of the iron is complete. Exp. 68, p. 77; trans. p. 111.

Further, Schinz, after examining critically the analyses of the gases of the blast furnace which were made by Bunsen and Ebelmen in 1839–40, and pointing out their insufficient accuracy, put the question, *What is the practical application of such analyses?* The answer given is almost the answer we give now, viz., that when we have an exact knowledge of the composition of the *charges*, it is possible to calculate from the analysis of the waste gases the amount of carbon which passes by direct reduction—reduction by solid carbon—into the gases, and which was therefore not burned at the twyres by the air of the blast.

This chapter is worthy of attentive study. Schinz concludes that the analysis of the waste gases is, even to the practical metallurgist, a valuable means of ascertaining what takes place inside his furnace in reference to the consumption of fuel.

The services of Schinz in enlarging and rectifying our notions of this important element of the theory of the blast furnace are not sufficiently recognized.

In the calculation of the calorific effects produced in the blast furnace, M. Schinz started with a fundamental *error* in the calculation of the production of heat by combustion of carbon to CO^2 and the reduction of CO^2 to CO. This error having been pointed out to him by M. Lührmann of Osnabrück, it was corrected in 1871, in Douglers' Journal, vol. 201, p. 231; but even there the correction is not perfectly satisfactory, as it imports into the subject the latent heat of gasification of carbon, about which nothing positive is known.

No injustice is therefore done in not entering on Schinz's *results* of calculation, which are further rendered useless by erroneous notions of the loss of caloric by radiation, etc., from the walls of the furnace.

And now we come to the present state of the theory of the blast furnace—that which gave rise to Mr. Gruner's Studies, and the foregoing translation.

Mr. Lowthian Bell, a hereditary iron-master, brought up from his youth in the midst of blast furnaces and great chemical works on the Tyne, and besides, having a thorough scientific education and a genial disposition to give freely all information he possessed, and to take kindly all given him by his neighbors and compeers in the trade, began in June, 1869, to contribute a series of papers to various Societies on the Chemical and Physical Phenomena of the Blast Furnace, which may be truly said to bring the theory in every respect to the actual level of the sciences of chemistry and physics, and to point the way to practical improvements, or at all events to put a scientific test of their working in the hands of furnace managers.*

Mr. Bell first examined the notion of "zones" of reaction in the furnace as used by Lampadius in his explanations of blast-furnace theory in 1838, afterwards adapted by Scheerer in 1853, and by Tunner later. He has constructed diagrams to scale of the results reported by these experimenters, as well as those obtained by Ebelmen in 1844 at Clerval with regard to reduction of the ores and the commencement of carburation. Practical men could thus for the first time see what the experiments had really ascertained, and that the lines of demarcation between the different "zones" were not meant as having any horizontal divisions or other very precise form. What Lampadius taught on this subject was that four or five changes took place—*pedetentim et graduatim*—in the descent of the charges against the ascent of the counter current of gases, and that there were zones in which these changes began and ended. Mr. Bell points out, that, as in practice a uniform descent of the materials in a furnace is interfered with by the difference in *size* and *specific gravity* of the ironstone, lime, and coke—by the friction of the sides of the furnace, more especially on the boshes, and by the mode

* *Journal of the Chemical Society*, June, 1869; *Report of the British Association*, etc., Exeter meeting, 1869; *Transactions of the Iron and Steel Institute*, 1869; *Journal of the Iron and Steel Institute*, 1870 to 1871.

of charging, whether central by a narrow tunnel-head, or all round as by a wide mouth—therefore the zones could not possibly have any shape such as given in Scheerer's work, and since repeated in books by several continental scientific metallurgists.* But it is also pretty certain that *zone* is a figurative expression for a region of change of temperature, change of reaction, etc.

However this may be, the examination of the notion of zones led Mr. Bell to make a series of direct experiments on reduction of ores by *the gases escaping from the blast furnaces*, and the true deduction from these experiments is that the reduction of calcined Cleveland and other ores, Fe^2O^3, is begun and ended by these gases at *a much lower temperature* than had been supposed proved by the experiments of Scheerer, Tunner, and Ebelmen, of those found by Schinz; for the temperature of the furnace gases, from Cleveland furnaces, of capacity varying from 6000 cubic feet to 26,000 cubic feet capacity, was seldom above 336° C., melting point of lead, and never above 450° C., the melting point of zinc. A certain size of the pieces of ore retards reduction, and even delays its commencement until sufficient heat is imparted, but the temperatures above given are, with *time*, sufficient to completely deoxidize ores of iron.†

Of all the substances found in "pig-iron"—and Fresenius

* *Metallurgie*, 1848 to 1853.

† The beginning and ending of the process of reduction was as follows:—

		Began.	Ended.
By Scheerer	.	400° C.	1000° to 1200°
Tunner	.	680°	1400°
Ebelmen	.	Below red heat.	Incipient fusion of ore.

See also, page 148, the experiments of Schinz.

made an analysis of a "Spiegel" iron of St. Louis near Marseilles, in which he found some twenty substances besides iron—and although no case occurs in which some two or three impurities do not occur, no substance is really essential to its constitution except *carbon.*

The circumstances which determine the union of this indispensable element with the metal are of high interest to the smelter, because upon the quantity and condition in which the carbon is associated with the iron depends, it is considered, the different qualities of the article he is manufacturing.

The portion of the furnace in which the combustion takes place, the temperature necessary for effecting it, and the exact source of immediate supply, have engaged the attention of all metallurgists who have studied the subject.

Scheerer says that carburation takes place only *after all traces* of unreduced oxide have disappeared, and where the temperature ranges from 1000° to 1600° Centigrade.

Tunner considered that his experiments proved that this combination takes place when the furnace has the temperature at which *cementation* takes place in steel furnaces, taken at 1150° Centigrade.

Mr. Bell, on the other hand, found that "an exposure of three hours to a temperature a little above the melting point of lead, and below that of zinc, sufficed to give a black deposit of carbon in a minute state of subdivision, so that he really believes it to be *combined* with the iron, or deposited by chemical action in such a form as to present great facilities for subsequent combination. It therefore seems probable that instead of the lowest and hottest portion of the furnace being the *zone of carburation*, this change occurs high up, where the temperature is comparatively low."* Foreign ores treated exactly as were the Cleveland ores in the gases of the furnaces, showed unmistakable signs of this carbon impregnation. And moreover, the *raw* iron-stone gave rise to a blacker and larger deposit than the *calcined*. The deposit was 1·68 per cent. of the iron in the ore in the calcined, and 4·63 per cent. on the raw ore, after each had been exposed twenty-four hours in the escaping gases.

In September and October, 1869, Mr. Bell read papers "On the Development and Appropriation of Heat in Iron Blast Furnaces of different Dimensions," before the members of the Iron and Steel Institute. In this paper there are explained all the principal elements of the *Calorific Phenomena* of the blast furnace; and many of the remarkable results worked out during succeeding years are given in a preliminary shape, sufficiently accurate to warrant the conclusion stated then, that a capacity of 11,000 to 12,000 cubic feet, and a height of 70 to 80 feet, is sufficient to realize all the economy it is possible to derive from this element of blast furnace engineering in *Cleveland circumstances.*

This paper was an appropriate introduction to the remarkable series of investigations presented to the Iron and Steel Institute at short intervals from 1870 to 1872, forming "an experimental and practical examination of the circumstances which determine the capacity of the blast furnace, the temperature of the blast, and the proper condition of the material to be operated upon."

* Mr. Bell found charcoal just as suitable for carburizing iron as precipitated carbon, but considers the latter *the most probable source* of the carbon of combination with the iron on account of the intimate mechanical mixture with the iron for its precipitation.

In the course of these researches, Mr. Bell completely filled up the details of what he had sketched out in reference to the chemical and physical theory of the blast furnace in 1869. If he has not exhausted the subject, he has at least left no point of the theory unexamined by all the light and methods of investigation of modern chemistry and physics. It only requires an examination of the headings of the forty-five sections of Mr. Bell's work to perceive how the minutest point has a section dedicated to it as conscientiously as is done for the most essential.

But the investigations which were made on the presence of alkaline cyanides in the blast furnace, in section xxvi., and on the part they play in the processes going on in the furnace, are so very important and interesting that I must attempt to give a summary of them.

Messrs. Bunsen and Playfair, in their "Report on the Gases evolved from Iron Furnaces, with reference to the theory of the Smelting of Iron"—made to the British Association at Cambridge in 1845—called attention to the fact that the gases from the lower part of the furnace, immediately over the point of entrance of the blast, contain cyanogen, which again disappears a short way above that point—so that at the top of the boshes* only traces of it are observed. And they remark, "The compound of this substance with potassium appears to play a most important part in the furnace, although its functions have apparently been altogether overlooked." Their detailed experiments led them to the conclusion that this cyanide of potassium owes its forma-

* The Alfreton furnace was 40·5 feet high, and 11 feet diameter at the widest.

tion to a direct union of carbon with potassium and nitrogen of the air.

Messrs. Bunsen and Playfair estimated—all corrections made—that in every cubic metre of gas at 2·75 feet above the twyrés there was to be found 8 to 10 grammes of cyanide of potassium.

Their experiments further showed that the cyanide of potassium is volatile at high temperatures. Thus, carried up by the ascending currents, it exerts its well-known *reducing* power—is thus decomposed into nitrogen, carbonic acid, and carbonate of potash—the gases passing off by the top, the potash falling back to the region where it is again converted into cyanide of potassium, under the influence of the carbon and nitrogen. "Hence a large quantity of ore may in this way be reduced in the lower part of the furnace by a comparatively small quantity of regenerated cyanide of potassium."

Dr. Percy,* in examining the figures given by Bunsen and Playfair, concludes, "that, unless the oxidation and regeneration of the cyanide of potassium takes place with a degree of rapidity hardly admissible, its service as a reducing agent must be so inappreciable that it may well have been 'previously entirely neglected.' "†

The phenomenon of a *decrease of oxygen*, as the gases leave the twyres, when compared with the atmospheric *nitrogen*, had been observed and an explanation proposed by Ebelmen. Dr. Percy‡ says, "such a decrease implies an abstraction of oxygen from the gaseous current, and its fixation in a solid state of combination, or an evolution of nitrogen in sensible

* *Op. cit.*, vol. ii. p. 451.

† Rep. B. A. 1845, p. 186.

‡ Vol. ii. pp. 444, 445.

quantity from the solid contents of the furnace; but I cannot understand how either of these results should occur:" and further on he writes, "I have failed to elicit from these analyses of gases any satisfactory general expressions such as might reasonably have been expected. I must, therefore, leave the reader to examine each 'table' for himself, and draw his own inferences therefrom."

But, as Mr. Bell observes, Dr. Percy makes no allusion to the alteration in the quantity of *carbon*, gauged by the same standard. Mr. Bell therefore selected four of the examples in the "tables," and these show incontestably that as a certain volume of gas ascends, it loses oxygen, but in addition to this, they prove that there is a simultaneous disappearance of carbon.

Mr. Bell gives the following statement of the loss of oxygen and carbon in the gases at 11½ feet above the twyres of an 80-feet Wear furnace:—

	Oxygen.	Carbon.
Example 1 . .	2·83 cwts.	1·37 cwt.
" 2 . .	3·19 "	1·80 "
" 3 . .	2·43 "	1·65 "
" 4 . .	2·51 "	1·91 "
Average	2·74 cwts.	1·62 cwt.

The undoubted disappearance of carbon from the gases of the furnace as they leave the hearth leads necessarily to inquire whether it may not throw some light on the simultaneous diminution in the quantity of oxygen.

"The form of combination into which the missing carbon has entered, I venture to suggest, is chiefly *cyanogen*, and possibly to some extent carbonic acid, both united with the alkaline metals, which I have shown abound in the lower region of the blast furnace." Mr. Bell then shows that there is much *probability* that the 1·62 cwt. of carbon, above ascertained as an *average*, assumes the form of 3·51 cwts. of cyanogen *per ton of iron yielded.* This assumes that about 40 grammes of cyanogen are present in the cubic metre of gases. (Dr. Percy's calculations were founded upon an analysis of Bunsen and Playfair giving only 4 grammes.) Admitting the probability that the carbon has assumed the form of cyanogen, it remains to consider in what way this action has led to a still more marked change in the quantity of oxygen, viz., 2·74 cwts. But even Mr. Bell fails to draw up any general theory which will fit every change which makes itself apparent in a blast furnace. These changes are well known to every intelligent manager to be numerous and sudden, and frequently take place without any apparent cause. The sum of all the evidence goes to show, that the *quantity* of cyanogen would account for the largest weight of carbon in excess which appeared at the twyres; and the presence of so large a quantity of cyanogen and alkaline gases appears to justify Mr. Bell's conclusion, "that it is to these substances that the apparent excess of carbon and oxygen in the lower region of the furnace has to be attributed."

Many other modes of reaction besides the direct union of C and N, in the presence of K and N, might be suggested as accounting for the disappearance of C and O from the gases, and Mr. Bell has illustrated this, p. 254 to 256, and we shall not enter upon the subject.

It is of great interest to record here Mr. Bell's own summary of what he "conceives to be the *action proper of the blast furnace*, *i. e.*, supposing no alkaline substance to be present.

This, no doubt, is a condition of things not to be found in practice, but experiment would indicate (*vide* section xxvi.) that the alkalies, along with their associated cyanogen, are not indispensable for the reduction and carburization of iron. This imaginary process would consist in the volatile constituents of the roasted ore, viz., its oxygen, being expelled probably before it has passed the first 10 or 12 feet of the furnace. This is inferred because already, at a depth of 16½ feet, there are only 2·06 cwts. of oxygen due to the minerals present in the gases, and of this 1·03, or something like it, has been contributed, not by Fe^2O^3, but by P^2O^5, SO^3, SiO^2 and CaO. The remainder, 1·03 cwts., along with a certain quantity of carbon, 0·34 cwt., is probably due to the carbonic acid of the flux, seeing that it requires a higher temperature to split up $CaCO^3$ than to reduce an oxide of iron. From the point B in the furnace (*vide* diagram, *example* of original 1) the oxygen in the gases remains almost stationary until we approach the twyres, where the small quantity of O absorbed by the iron in the dissociation of CO, and that combined with the P, S, Si, and Ca, found in the iron and slag, alone ought to appear. Here also the quantity of carbon in the gases ought to be that furnished by the coke, less the portion which may have been carried off by the reduction of CO^2 to CO in the manner already described."

"Simultaneously with the process of reduction is the deposition of carbon by the splitting up of CO into C and CO^2, and that this takes place very soon after the immersion of the ironstone among the gases, seems to admit of no doubt. This operation of carbon-impregnation will continue until the iron or its lower oxide is sufficiently heated to suspend further action, in the manner already fully explained in the sections upon the dissociation of CO."

"No doubt, even in this supposititious case of the absence of the alkalies K^2O and Na^2O, there would ensue irregularities in the composition of the gases at the same position in the furnace, which might result from a retarded or accelerated rate of reduction, from the nature of the ore itself, or from some of those mechanical causes which have been spoken of. Substantially, however, I apprehend there would not be found any of those discrepancies, to explain which I have bestowed some pains, and which, in my judgment, are to be entirely attributed to the presence of the alkalies, potash and soda, and the consequent generation of cyanogen."

"If I am correct in this supposition, and if the experimental proof of the great fluctuations in the quantities of these substances is to be relied upon, it is not difficult to comprehend that there must necessarily be corresponding irregularities in the character of the products in different parts of the furnace."

Such is the explanation of the action proper of the blast furnace in 1873. The generation that has lived since Lampadius taught has seen such precision given to the expression of the chemical phenomena going on in this vast apparatus as takes it out of the domain of empiricism, and puts it into that of exact science.

But it was not till 1870 that the phenomenon of *dissociation* of carbonic oxide—the splitting up of CO, so that 2 CO is transformed into CO^2 + C—was discovered, and that all the conditions of this phenomenon were examined experimentally and described. Though Mr. Schinz had observed the deposit of carbon, and had applied the facts to explain carburation, he gave no explanation of its origin.

From Mr. Bell's experiments it seems highly probable that *carbon impregnation*, as he terms the action, by the splitting up or dissociation of CO, takes place at nearly as low a temperature as desoxidation, which, in the case of Cleveland calcined ore is *begun* at 200° to 210° C. (section xi. p. 46). And as the extent of reduction in different ores is affected apparently by their molecular condition (section iv. pp. 17–19), when submitted under perfectly similar circumstances to the action of CO; so the same irregularity in the extent to which *carbon impregnation* takes place has been observed for different ores. Generally speaking, the more readily an ore or oxide of iron loses its oxygen, the more capable it is of dissociating carbon from CO.

Very small differences of temperature greatly affect the quantity of *carbon* yielded by the CO.

In experiment 211 (p. 48), 100 Fe in calcined Cleveland ore, at a temperature *not visibly red*, the carbon deposited in $4\frac{1}{2}$ hours was 64·0 C. Using the same ore the following figures were obtained:—

		Carbon deposited.
Exp. 228.	Temperature for 11 hours *red* and 10 hours *bright red*—in all 21 hours .	2·3 % of Fe.
" 229.	Temperature *very bright red* for $6\frac{1}{2}$ hours	0·3 " "

Practically it may be assumed that the phenomenon of carbon impregnation diminishes very rapidly as soon as a *red heat* is reached. The temperature most favorable for its production is between 400° C. and 450° C. But if the ores with carbon deposited at this temperature be only partially reduced, and exposed to a *bright red* heat, the carbon will be consumed to the extent at least of the supply of oxygen in the unreduced portion of the ore. It remains therefore a question whether all the carbon necessary to constitute the various qualities of pig-iron is the result of carbon impregnation accompanying the process of reduction in the upper portion of the furnace, or whether a portion is derived from the *incandescent carbon of the hearth.*

The only other point on which it seems useful for me here to attempt to give the results of Mr. Bell's investigations, is that of the behavior of *limestone* in the blast furnace—its use as a *flux*, and its use for removing sulphur in Cleveland ores. On this latter point it has been proved that these ores may be used *without lime*, but then the "pig" contained much more sulphur than when lime was used, viz., 0·33 %, and the *quality* in point of strength suffered considerable deterioration.

But the most interesting question in reference to the limestone is, What becomes of the carbonic acid united to the lime? The use of $CaO\ CO^2$, as a flux, is the usual means by which CO^2 finds its way into the blast furnace. The CO^2 which we find in the gases owes its origin, be it repeated, to the expulsion of that contained in the limestone, to the desoxidation of the ore, and to *carbon deposition* by the reaction so fully described. Mr. Bell concludes, from experiments directed to this point in section xxi., that as carbonic acid in an atmosphere of CO^2 is only sparingly given off at a full red heat, and CO^2 commences to undergo decomposition at 400° to 500° C., all the CO^2 entering the furnace combined with CaO, *leaves it as CO*, and adds, "this view of what really takes place in the furnaces in the Cleveland district is further confirmed by the fact that the CO^2 in the gases never exceeds that due to reduction of Fe^2O^3, and to the dissociation of that portion of CO which furnishes the carbon found in the pig-iron." In opposition to this conclusion the note at foot of p. 65 of M. Gruner's "Studies" must be referred to, where it is proved that in the special example of a Clarence furnace the $0^{lb}\cdot058$ of carbon absorbed to transform CO^2 into CO is less than the $0^{lb}\cdot082$ of carbon in the limestone. The experiments are very difficult to make with such precision that well-defined *conclusions can be drawn* (see Bell, section xxi. p. 110, note).

The application of the phenomenon of dissociation and of the decomposition of the CO^2 in the limestone takes place in estimating the *quantity of caloric required in the process of iron-smelting.* Mr. Bell's services in this part of the theory of the blast furnace are unique. His papers on the subject have been translated into German by P. Tunner, into Swedish by Rinman, and the work of M. Gruner testifies to the interest it has excited in France. Bell's experiments, showing the reactions that take place between the oxides of iron and iron itself, and the CO and CO^2 of the gases of the furnace, demonstrate the fallacy of calculating the calorific efficiency of the fuel in a blast furnace upon the supposition that it can all be resolved into CO^2, as was done before the Institution of Mechanical Engineers in November, 1868, and afterwards in January, 1869. They prove that we must content ourselves with ascertaining to what extent the carbon applied in a furnace can be made to assume its highest state of oxidation, for which it produces 3·28 times as much caloric as when it takes only the lower state—that is, Mr. Bell first proved that the proportion of $\frac{CO^2}{CO}$ in the blast furnace gases is the *index of the calorific efficiency* of the furnace. After the complete manner in which this proposition has been demonstrated in M. Gruner's text, it is quite unnecessary to refer to it further. This point is no longer questioned, although it is often overlooked by persons taking part in "discussions" of papers on the limit of the economy of fuel in blast furnaces. There is in fact only one rational way of estimating the quantity of heat required in the process of iron-smelting. There are questions open as to the values to be given to certain factors, to certain experimental data, but there should be no question as to the *principle* of calculation which is alone available. There should be no question now as to the *principle* of calculation of the heat *received* and *developed* in a furnace, nor of the heat *absorbed* in the chemical action and in fusion, and carried off by radiation and reaction from the walls and foundations of the furnace, in the twyre water, and in the sensible heat of the escaping gases.

Some years ago calculations were put forward for determining the consumption of fuel by another method.

Various assumptions were made, for instance that it *is impossible* to have a greater proportion of CO^2 to CO in the gases of a blast furnace than $\frac{1}{5}$ CO^2 to $\frac{4}{5}$ CO, when the CO^2 of the limestone is eliminated—*i.e.* an assumption at variance with almost all experience of furnaces of fair proportions and in good working order—as, for example, the six furnaces examined in this book, in which the proportions (after elimination of CO^2 of limestone) are

$$\frac{1}{4} \quad \frac{1}{2{\cdot}73} \quad \frac{1}{3{\cdot}55} \quad \frac{1}{3{\cdot}4} \quad \frac{1}{2{\cdot}19} \quad \text{and} \quad \frac{1}{2{\cdot}9}$$

respectively. The proportions of limestone (carbonate of lime) for these examples being in cwts. to the ton of iron,

16 13·5 12·5 8 8 18

whilst the proportions in the calculations in question were taken at 8 to 10 cwts.

But the assumption that the CO^2 of the limestone passes off entirely as such in the gases is gratuitous. It is still an open question.

It is assumed further, that it is by the caloric due to *this composition* of the gases $\frac{CO^2}{CO} = \frac{1}{4}$ (calculated at 6000° Fahrenheit units), that all the *calorific effects* in the furnace are produced, viz., the fusion of the iron and the slags, and also the chemical effects of reduction—which assumptions are erroneous: for the composition of the gases is an effect of reduction, and not a cause. The reasoning in the context, moreover, is, *that the fixed oxygen in the ore has to be made to enter into combination with the fixed carbon in the coke*, and that therefore, because it has been found "practically" that when a mixture of ore and carbon is exposed in a close retort to the heat of the furnace, it is necessary to supply a large amount of heat in order to bring about a combination of the elements—which is no doubt true—it is calculated that for the reduction of the peroxide of iron, there is an excess of heat *absorbed* requiring as much as 3·19 cwts. of carbon to compensate it. This is a conclusion at variance with the direct experiments quoted in detail, p. 49, showing that there is very nearly a balance between the heat developed by burning CO to CO^2 in the process of reduction, and the heat absorbed in effecting the reduction, that is, in effecting the *disengagement of the oxygen* from the *iron* in the ores.

Then again the specific heat of iron is taken as 0·12, water being 1. This is the specific heat of *bar iron* at temperatures of about 250° C. For such "temperature" as is assumed for the fusion of the iron (viz. 2223° C. or 4000° F.), the specific heat of pig-iron is quite problematical. If such a degree of temperature as 2200° C. exists in the hearth, the specific heat of the molten iron would be 0·22 (see Table 6, Note VI., Appendix). And further, the specific heat of slags is taken as 0·20, but the specific heat at the temperature assumed in the calculations in question, 4000° F. = 2223 C., would be 0·40, according to the experiments and calculations of M. Schinz.

Thus, admitting the principle of the calculation as to caloric required for fusion of iron and slags, *the factors used* are so arbitrarily chosen, that the results have no accordance with direct experiment, no scientific accuracy, no practical value. That a result something near what might be expected is finally obtained, is only an illustration of Mr. Canning's sarcastic remark, "that anything can be proved by figures."

This too is the place to notice some criticisms of Mr. Bell's conclusions as to the use and abuse of a superheated blast.

On the theoretical opposition to Mr. Bell's conclusions, nothing need be said. However, a paper entitled "Further Results from the use of Hot Blast Firebrick Stoves" contains two tables of the working of two Consett furnaces examined by Mr. Bell, from which tables of results conclusions are drawn, which an examination of them without preconceived notions does not justify.

At the bottom of one table (No. IV. Furnace) is written:

Decrease of temperature, 200°. Increase of coke per ton, 213 lbs.

and at the bottom of the other (No. V. Furnace):

Mean decrease of temperature, 200°. Mean increase of coke per ton, 169 lbs.

Now, taking the period of working at the blast temperatures of

	cwts.	qrs.	lbs.
1400° F. = 763° C., the mean consumption of coke is	17	3	6
1200° F. = 650° C., the consumption . .	18	1	19
Therefore the increased consumption for loss of 200°	0	2	15

or 71 lbs.—exactly $\frac{1}{3}$ of the estimate stated.

Again, the difference of consumption of coke when working at 1400° F. varies, so that the greatest difference is 123 lbs., or nearly double the difference for a *fall* of 200° F. The difference between the *greatest* consumption at 1400° and the consumption at 1200° is only 67 lbs.

The difference when the furnace is working with blast at 1200°, and at 1190°, or a fall of 10°, is 194 lbs. coke, or 2·7 times as great as for a fall of 200°.

For the same temperature of blast, viz., 1148° at two periods, the difference was 82 lbs. of coke, or more than for the fall from 1400° to 1200°.

For No. V. Furnace the facts are:

For the furnace working at blast temperatures of 1450° F. = 788 C., the difference at one period and another is 90 lbs.

Working at 1260° F., or a fall of 190° F., the difference is 128 lbs. (in favor of hot blast).

	cwt.	qrs.	lbs.	
Again, the mean consumption at 1450° =	19	3	25	
" " " 1250 =	21	1	21	
	1	2	24	= 192 lbs.

Thus in the one furnace a fall of 10° increases the consumption by 194 lbs., and in the other a fall of 200° increases it by 192 lbs.

If we take into consideration the very great variations in *weight of blast* at the time one "consumption" was taken and that at the other, the difference of yield from one period to the other, and from one furnace to the other, the conclusion drawn from these extracts from the books of the Consett Company as to the greater economy of a blast at 760° C. and the one at 650° C. cannot be accepted as proving that there is any necessary connection between the difference of consumption of coke, and it is only by *selecting results* that the difference of 2 Cent. increases for the decrease of temperature of 200° F. = 160 C. can be made out for particular weeks of working.

Upon the value of such deductions from "facts" as this paper contains, the following quotation from section xxxii. of Mr. Bell's work gives a practical iron-master's estimate: "There is nothing easier than to persuade ourselves that this or the other furnace is doing better or worse than some other with which it is compared, or in comparing the same furnace at different periods. In such an inquiry it is absolutely indispensable that all disturbing causes should be eliminated, and every instance brought down to one common level in respect to the coke, ironstone, and limestone consumed, temperature of the blast, and every other circumstance connected with its working."

The opinion to which all the evidence of fact and calculation leads appears to me to be, that it is more economical to get the *necessary caloric* by a *good design* of the furnace than by a superheated blast.

Reverting further to Mr. Bell's work, it is of some importance to state here the values of the *factors* of calorific effects, used by Mr. Bell and M. Gruner respectively, in the calculation of the caloric necessary for, or absorbed in, the production of iron; and to make the subject more distinct, the weight of materials per ton of iron yielded, of *Mr. Bell's example, Section xli., p.* 374, *are used.*

	Mr. Bell's			M. Gruner's	
	Factors.	Materials, Tons.	Calories.	Factors.	Calories.
Reduction of Fe^2O^3 of iron . .	1780	0·93	1665	1887	1750
Reduc. of P^2O^5, SO^3 and SiO^2 .	170	...	170	210	210
Fusion of Pig Iron	330	1·00	330	330	330
Fusion of Slags	550	1·396	770	550	770
Decomposition of Limestone . .	370	0·55	202	3735	203
Decomp. of H^2O in Blast per lb.	3400	0·0025	85	3222	80
Carbon Impregnation	2400	0·003	72	0	0
Decomp. of CO^2 in Limestone .	3200	0·066	206	0	0
Transmission through walls of furnace, twyre, water, etc. .	270	...	270	270	270
Expansion of Blast	185	...	185	0	0
			3955		3613

Thus, there are three sources of *absorption* which together involve 463 calories per lb. of iron produced, which Mr. Bell deems it necessary to take into calculation, and which M. Gruner does not. The question of the decomposition of CO^2 in limestone has been referred to above. The "Expansion of the Blast" introduces an element of guess-work for which it is difficult to find a reason. Upon the final balance of accounts Mr. Bell has 337 calories more than M. Gruner for this special case—a difference of 8·5 %.

On the other hand, for the caloric evolved on the supposition that $\frac{CO^2}{CO} = 0{\cdot}783$ (p. 378), M. Gruner is agreed with Mr. Bell on the principle of calculation for every element but one, viz., the effect of the CO^2 of the limestone.

Mr. Bell reckons			M. Gruner reckons		
C in CO of Gases . .	13·22		C in CO of Gases . .	13·22	13·22
Less that in Limestone	1·32				
		11·90	C in CO^2 of Gases . .	6·58	
C in CO^2 of Gases		6·58	Less that in Limestone	1·32	5·26
Total C in Gases . .		18·48	Total		18·48

And reducing both to one unit we have

	C.	Cals.	C.	Cals.
C in CO	0·595 × 2473 =	1465	0·661 × 2473 =	1635
C in CO^2	0·329 × 8080 =	2660	0·263 × 8080 =	2135
		4125		3770

Thus, M. Gruner's estimate of the heat evolved is 8 % *less* than Mr. Bell's, arising from difference of appreciation of the function of the CO^2 of the limestone in the blast furnace.

As to the sensible heat carried off in the gases, the estimates would be the same, viz., 430 of the lb. units.

As to the caloric carried in by the blast, or rather as to the balance of calories for heating the blast, the calculations give 253 calories in the one and 278 in the other, or the temperature of blast would have to be 220° in the one case and 240° in the other.

But the true principles of calorific determinations are so exhaustively displayed in M. Gruner's Studies, that I must refer those who desire to familiarize themselves with these principles and their applications to that source of information, and especially to sections 4 and 16 to 21.

Before concluding this note, however, let us examine one case to illustrate the necessity of attending to all the "vital statistics" of furnaces before drawing any conclusions as to their technical economy.

Let us take for example Clarence furnace 1866 and Consett No. 4.

ANALYSIS OF TECHNICAL ECONOMY, ETC.

	Clarence.	Consett, No. 4.	Ratios.	Remarks.
Height in feet	80	55	1 to 1·45	
Capacity in cubic feet	11500	10300	1 to 1·115	
Ore per ton Iron yielded	2·440	2·083	Iron 41 % to	
Limestone do.	0·683	0·406	48 %	* Ratio of total to smelt to total carbon = 1 to 1.
Ash in Coke	0·088	0·076		
Total raw material to smelt	3·211	2·565	1·28 to 1*	
Pig-iron yielded in 24 h.	38·6	60	1·55 to 1	† Carbon burned at Twyres, or for smelting, *plus* that due to greater amount of *caloric carried in*, comes to within 4·5 p. c. of the ratio 1 to 1, compared with total weight smelted.
Cubic feet capacity per ton	300	171	1·75 to 1	
Weight of Blast, tons	5·193	3·75		
Weight of Gases	6·933	5·161		
Total Coke, tons	1·115	0·900		
Total Carbon	0·990	0·789	1·26 to 1*	
Carbon burned at Twyres	0·930	0·675	1·37 to 1†	
Temperature of Blast	485°	718°		
Caloric carried in by Blast, cals.	602	643	1 to 1·07†	The caloric carried off is as nearly as may be in the ratio of the *carbon consumed for reduction*.
Temperature of Gases	332°	248°		
Caloric carried off by Gases, cals.	545	303	1·80 to 1	
Carbon burned in Zone of Reduction	0·058	0·113	1 to 1·95	

This table shows that in a *technical* point of view there is no practical difference in the economy of working in the two furnaces. The greater yield of the Consett furnace is another question. *The rate of driving*, calculated by the capacity of furnace *per ton of yield*, is as 1·75 for Consett against 1 at Clarence. Why one furnace can be driven faster than another is as yet unexplained. At Cleveland the pressure of the blast was 2·75 lbs. as at Consett, but the area of the twyres at Consett was 80 square inches, while at Clarence it was 50. 80 is to 50 as 1·60 to 1, but it would require 80 to 46, to give the ratio of faster driving, viz., 1·75 to 1. This is a subject well worthy the attention of iron-masters and their managers.

It will not be without interest to mention here, in reference to the economy of fuel in blast furnaces, that the recorded consumption of *coal* per ton of forge iron produced has been, at the Dowlais Ironworks, as given on the authority of the late Mr. Truran by Dr. Percy, and as given by Mr. Menelaus, the present manager of these vast works, as follows:—

	In 1791.	1831.	1862.
In Furnace . .	6 tons. 6 cwt. 0 qrs.	2 10 0	1 8 0
For Engine . .	1 15 0	0 10 0	0 0 0
Calcining . . .	0 6 0	0 6 0	0 5 0
Total Coal . .	9 7 0	3 6 0	1 13 0
or of *Coke* . .	6 5 0	2 4 0	1 2 0
or of *Carbon* .	5 10 0	1 19 0	0 19 1 12 lbs.

Or in three successive generations as 5 : 2 : 1.

Again, let us call to mind that

	Carbon.	
Consett No. 4 furnace works with . .	15·78 cwt.	with 48 % ores.
Clarence	19·8	40 "
Pousin (capacity 4080 ft.)	19·4	41 "
Consett No. 5	20·0	48 "
Osnabrück (Georg-Marienhutte) (C=8040)	25·5	24 "

These are a few illustrations to prove that the minimum quantity of fuel required can only be determined approximately for each particular case, *of which all the vital statistics are known. Capacity, height, temperature of blast, are all subordinate to design of furnace, quality of material*, and skill in management.

The history of the hot blast—the different apparatus for applying it—its effects on the progress of iron manufacture—and its theory, I feel reluctantly obliged to reserve for further consideration.

NOTE VI.—USEFUL TABLES AND MEMORANDA FOR CALCULATIONS OF BLAST FURNACE PHENOMENA.

1. *Chemical Equivalents, etc.*

Substances.	Formula or Symbol.	Atomic Weight O. S.	Atomic Weight N. S.	Specific Gravity. Air = 1.	Specific Gravity. Water = 1.
Carbon . . .	C	6	12	...	...
Oxygen . . .	O	8	16	1·108	...
Nitrogen . . .	N	14	14	0·969	...
Phosphorus . .	P	31	31	...	1·77
Silicon . . .	Si	14	21	...	...
Hydrogen . .	H	1	2	0·0694	...
Sulphur . . .	S	32	32	2·216*	2·03
Calcium . . .	Ca	20	40	...	1·58
Aluminium . .	Al	13·7	275	...	2·67
Iron	Fe or Fe^2	28	56	...	7·79
Carbonic Oxide	CO	14	28	0·969	...
" Acid .	CO^2	22	44	1·524	...
Water. . . .	HO or H^2O	9	18	...	1·00
Silica	Si O^2	30	37	...	2·65
Phosphoric Acid	P^2 O^5	102	142	...	...
Alumina . . .	Al^2 O^3	79	103	...	3·90
Calcia or Lime .	Ca O	48	56	...	...
Limestone (pure)	CaO CO^2	70	100	...	2·72

* *as vapor.*

Composition of Air.			
By Volume.		By Weight.	
Air O + N.		O + N	
20·96	79·24	23·31	76·68
or in round numbers 21	79	23	77

Weight of cubic metre of air, 1·300 kilo.

Weight of cubic foot = 0·06985 lb. ∴ 1 lb = ~~14·35~~ cubic feet of dry air.

Air in winter contains about ·0000342 lbs. per cubic foot, or, 0·00495 lbs. per lb. of dry air.

FOR C AND O.

	Equiv. Weight.	Per cent.		Volume.	Sp. gr.
C	12 or 6	42·86	Carbon Vapor	1	0·82922
O	16 or 8	57·14	Oxygen Gas	1	1·10563
CO	28 or 14	100·00	Carbonic Oxide	2	1·93485
1 Equiv. Carbonic oxide = CO = 14 . .				1	0·96742

FOR CO^2.

	Equiv. Weight.	Per cent.				
C	12 or 6	27·27	Carbon Vapor (?)	1	0·82922	
2 O	32 or 16	72·73	Oxygen Gas	2	2·21126	
	44 or 22	100·00		2	3·04048	Regnault,
[1 Equivalent CO^2 = 22.]				1	1·52024	1·52910

For Iron Ores.

The natural combinations of iron with oxygen are,

1. Suboxide of iron and peroxide	$\left.\begin{matrix} Fe \\ Fe^2 \end{matrix}\right\\}$ O 4	with 72·4 % iron.
2. Oxide of iron or peroxide	$Fe^2 H^6 O^3$	with 70 % iron.
3. Hydrated oxide of iron	$\left.\begin{matrix} H \\ Fe^2 \end{matrix}\right\\} O^9$	with 60 % iron.
4. Carbonate of protoxide	$Fe\,CO^3$	with 48·3 % iron.

2. *Caloric.—Determination of Caloric of Combustion.*

Carbon.

1 lb. CO to CO^2 = 2403 calories by experiment.

1 lb. C to CO^2 = 8080 do. do.

1 lb. carbon gives $\frac{7}{3}$ lbs. CO.

$\therefore \frac{7}{3}$ CO burned gives $\frac{7}{3} \times 2403 = 5607$.

Hence, for the combustion of 1 lb. C to CO we have

$8080 - 5607 = 2473$ calories by calculation.

Iron.

	Cals.		
1 lb. iron burned to $Fe^3 O^4$ (magnetic oxide) gives	1648,	Dulong . ∵ Fe^2O^3	=1854
" " "	1575,	Pouillet, . ∵ "	=1775
" " "	1582,	Andrews, "	=1780
" to Fe O (protoxide)	=1352	Favre and Silbermann, "	=2028
			7437
The mean of which experiments and calculation			=1859

Number adopted by M. Gruner is 1887

Mr. Bell, 1780

Thermometers.

9° Fahrenheit = 5° Centigrade = 4° Reaumur.

$$\text{Temperature Fahrenheit} = \frac{9}{5}\ \text{Temp. Cent.} + 32$$

$$\text{" "} = \frac{9}{4}\ \text{Reau.} + 32$$

$$\text{Temperature Centigrade} = \frac{5}{9}\ (\text{Temp. Fahr.} - 32) = \frac{5}{6}\ \text{Temp. Reau.}$$

Quantities of Heat

are expressed in units of weights of water heated one degree, or in pounds of water heated one degree of Fahrenheit (the British unit); or in kilogrammes of water, one degree of Centigrade (the French unit); or, as in this translation, in pounds of water raised one degree Centigrade.

One Centigrade unit of heat equals 1·8 Fahrenheit units for same unit of weight of water.

Thermometric Pyrometer Scales.

Supposing we have determined the *Freezing Point* and *Boiling Point* of thermometers or pyrometers of iron, glass, copper, and platina, these thermometers show at 300°, by the *air thermometer* or true temperature, as follows:—

Air.	Platina.	Copper.	Glass.	Iron.
300.	312.	329.	353.	373.

How vague, therefore, must be thermometric units as determined for higher temperatures still!

3. *Melting Points, Latent Heat, etc.*

1. Experiments of Person.

	Melting-point Degrees. C.	Specific Heat.		Latent Heat.
		Solid.	Fluid.	
Tin	237·7	0·0562	0·0637	14·25
Bismuth	266·8	0·0308	0·0363	12·64
Lead	326·2	0·0314	0·0402	5·37
Zinc	415·0	0·0955	...	28·13

	Daniell.	Pouillet.
Gold	1250	1102
Silver	1100	1023

Iron.

	Pouillet.	Plattner.	Blast Furnace Slags.	
			Plattner.	
			Temperature of Formation of Slag.	Melting point of Slags when formed.
English Hammered	1600° C.			
Soft, French	1500			
Steel, best	1400			
Steel	1300			
Gray Pig-iron	1200	1530 C.		
White Pig-iron	1050	?	1876° C.	1445° C.

12

Mitscherlich (*Chemie*, vol. i. p. 289) reckons the melting point of *platinum* at *under* 1560° C.; and if this be a true deduction, then certainly the melting points of gold, silver, iron, etc., as above given, are too high. *There is no certainty in these melting points* being exact.

4. *Specific Heats of Gases*, Water = 1.

	Equal Weights.	Equal Volumes.	
Atmospheric Air . .	0·2377	0·2377	These numbers for equal volumes are so nearly the same that it seems highly probable that for permanent gases the specific heat of *equal volumes* is the same.—*Regnault.*
Oxygen	0·2182	0·2412	
Hydrogen	0·4046	0·2356	
Nitrogen	0·2440	0·2370	
Carbonic Oxide . .	0·2479	0·2399	
Carbonic Acid . .	0·2164	0·3308	
Steam	0·4750	0·2950	

5. *Specific Heats of Solids.*

The specific heat of bodies varies with the specific gravity. Thus—

Regnault found Charcoal . . .	0·2415
Coal	0·2009
Diamond . . .	0·1469

Dulong and Petit found that the specific heat varies with the temperature.

Substances.	Mean Specific Heat.	
	Between 0° and 100°.	Between 0° and 300°.
Iron (rod)	0·1098	0·1218
Zinc	0·0927	0·1015
Silver	0·0557	0·0611
Platinum	0·0335	0·0355
Glass	0·177	0·190

The specific heat varies from the solid state to the fluid. Thus—

	Solid.	Fused 350° to 450°.
Lead . .	·0314	0·402

6. *Schinz's Experimental Results on Specific Heats.*

	Specific Gravities.		lbs. per C. Ft.	Specific Heat at 100°.	Increase for each 100°.
IRON.					
Gray Foundry Iron . .	6·635	7·275	471 mean	0·09049	0·00399
Light Gray	6·916	7·572	495	...	...
White and "Spiegel" .	7·056	7·889	502	0·08937	0·00635
Steel (Cementation) . .	7·400	7·825	522	...	...
Cast Steel	7·826	8·092	...	...	...
Bar Iron	7·352	7·912	...	0·1190	...
Wire	7·794	8·100	...	...	...
Coke	1·120	...	75	0·1571	0·0194
ORES.					
Calcareous Iron Ore . .	2·503	...	168	0·2557	...
Red Spathose, raw . .	3·679	...	249	0·11174	0·084
" calcined .	4·413	...	296	0·153006	0·013
White Spathose, raw .	3·555	...	242	0·12478	0·045
" calcined	4·460	...	305	0·17955	0·008
Clay Iron Stone, raw .	3·238	...	218	0·1894	0·0033
" calcined	3·829	...	256	0·17632	0·0141
Magnetic Ore	4·220	...	284	0·16674	0·0071
Limestone, uncalcined .	2·525	...	172	...	...
" calcined . .	2·075	...	140	...	...
Blast Furnace Slags . .	2·383	...	160	0·1469	0·010
Do. do.	2·917	...	195	0·1479	0·0116
Do. do.	2·777	...	156	0·1492	0·0117
Do. Hayange .	2·573	...	176	0·14698	0·0125

Memorandum.—Average weight, per cubic foot, of the materials of the charges, as they are filled into the charging barrows at *Clarence Works*:—

Coke . .	·218 cent.	= 24·5 lbs.	= $\frac{1}{3}$ of theoretical or solid.		
Calcined Ore .	·678 "	= 76·5 "	= $\frac{1}{3}$	"	"
Limestone .	·607 "	= 68 "	= $\frac{1}{2.6}$	"	"

Memorandum.—If a weight m of a substance be heated to temperature t', and plunged in a weight m of water, raising the temperature thereof by t degrees, then s, the specific heat, is determined by the equation $sm't' = mt \therefore s = \frac{mt}{mt'}$.

From this equation we have also $t'' = \frac{mt}{sm'}$.

For example, a platina ball, of 200 grains weight, heated in a furnace, plunged into a weight of water of 1000 grains, raises the temperature of the water by 7°; then $m = 1000 - m' = 200 t = 7 - s$ (spec. heat of platina) = 0·0355 (?)

$$t' = \frac{1000 \times 7}{200 \times \cdot 0355} = \frac{7000}{7 \cdot 1} = 976^\circ \text{ C.}$$

Here the supposition is made that the sp. heat of platina is the same at 976° as at 300; but, supposing the difference for the first 200°, viz., 0·002 or for 100° = 0·001 to contain these at 976, or say 900°, we should have 0·001 × (900 — 300) = 0·006. Then 0·0355 + 0·006 = 0·0415,

$$\text{and therefore } \frac{1000 \times 7}{200 \times 0 \cdot 061} = \frac{7000}{8 \cdot 2} = 854^\circ,$$

a difference of 122°.

The most recent experiments are those of Professor Wanhold of Chemnitz, and from these, made with every precaution to insure accuracy, the specific heat of platinum may be taken for pyrometric work as *constant*.

INDEX.

Formulae

a = Carbon in fuel

b = Carbon in CO^2 of charge $= \frac{3}{11} CO^2$

c = Carbon in the pig

p = Carbon in the gas $= a + b - c$ or $= \frac{3}{7} y + \frac{3}{11} my$

Q = Heat required from the fuel $+ 8080\,b$

$m = \frac{CO^2}{CO} = \frac{11}{7}\left(\frac{Q - 2473\,p}{8080\,p - Q}\right)$

y = Weight of CO in gas $= \frac{77\,p}{33 + 21\,m}$ or $= \frac{7}{3}\left(\frac{8080\,p - Q}{5607}\right)$

my = Do CO^2 " Do $= m \times y$ or $= \frac{11}{3}\left(\frac{Q - 2473\,p}{5607}\right)$

d = Oxygen in Metals reduced + Oxygen in CO^2 of the charge =

$\frac{3}{7}$* Fe in pig $+ \frac{8}{7}$ Si in pig $+ \frac{40}{31}$ P in pig + Mn in pig + S in pig $+ \frac{8}{3} b$

x = Oxygen in the blast including moisture $= p\left(\frac{44 + 56\,m}{33 + 21\,m}\right) - d$

Weight of Blast including moisture $= 4.256\,x$

N = Do Nitrogen in Blast $= 3.253\,x$

Heat from combustion of Carbon in fuel to $CO^2 = \frac{3}{11} my - b \times 8080$

Do Do Do to $CO = \frac{3}{7} y \times 2473$

Carbon burned to CO in zone of reduction $= \left(\frac{9}{28}^{*} Fe + \frac{6}{7} Si + \frac{30}{31} P + S + Mn \text{ in pig}\right) = f$ +
$b - \frac{3}{11} my$

CO burned to CO^2 in Do $= \frac{7}{3}\left(\frac{3}{11} my - b\right)$

Carbon burned to CO in zone of fusion $= a - c - b - f + \frac{3}{11} my$

Oxygen in dry air of the blast $= .9768\,x$

Weight of dry air of Do $= 4.23\,x$

Do moisture of Do $= 4.23\,x \times .0062$

Carbon in CO of Gas $= \frac{3}{7} y$

Do in CO^2 of Do $= \frac{3}{11} my$

* $\frac{3}{7}$ for Fe^2O^3 and $\frac{2}{7}$ for FeO — * $\frac{9}{28}$ for Fe^2O^3 and $\frac{3}{14}$ for FeO

		Factors Gruner	Bell
A. Reduction of Fe in pig	Wgt. of Fe in pig from Fe_2O_3	1887.	1780
Do	Do Do " " FeO	1258.	1187
Do Si "	Do Si "	7000.	8000
Do P "	Do P "	5767.	5747
Do S "	Do S "	2560.	2500
Do Mn "	Do Mn "		
Fusion of pig	Do pig #1, 2 & 3	337.	330
	#4 & 5		
	White		
(Carbon impregnation)	Do C "		2400.
B Decomposition of Carbonate	Do Carbonate	373.5	370
(Do of CO_2)	Do C in CO_2		3200
Fusion of Slag	Do Slag if bassic	550.	550
	if acid	500.	
C Evaporation of H_2O and Vol. in chge	Do H_2O + Vol.	606.5	540
D Decomposition of H_2O in Blast	Do Blast x .0062	3222.	3778
E Carried off by the gas	Do Gas x Temp. in Deg. C	.237	.239
F. Radiation through walls			183
by tuyere water		400.	91
Expansion of Blast			187

Heat Produced per Gruner

From the Blast	Wgt. of Blast x Temp in Deg C	.239
Do Fuel to CO_2	Do C in CO_2	8080.
Do Do CO	Do C " CO	2473.

CATALOGUE

OF

Practical and Scientific Books

PUBLISHED BY

HENRY CAREY BAIRD & CO.

INDUSTRIAL PUBLISHERS, BOOKSELLERS AND IMPORTERS,

810 Walnut Street, Philadelphia.

☞ Any of the Books comprised in this Catalogue will be sent by mail, free of postage, to any address in the world, at the publication prices.

☞ A Descriptive Catalogue, 84 pages, 8vo., will be sent free and free of postage, to any one in any part of the world, who will furnish his address.

☞ Where not otherwise stated, all of the Books in this Catalogue are bound in muslin.

AMATEUR MECHANICS' WORKSHOP:

A treatise containing plain and concise directions for the manipulation of Wood and Metals, including Casting, Forging, Brazing, Soldering and Carpentry. By the author of the "Lathe and Its Uses." Seventh edition. Illustrated. 8vo. $3.00

ANDRES.—A Practical Treatise on the Fabrication of Volatile and Fat Varnishes, Lacquers, Siccatives and Sealing Waxes.

From the German of ERWIN ANDRES, Manufacturer of Varnishes and Lacquers. With additions on the Manufacture and Application of Varnishes, Stains for Wood, Horn, Ivory, Bone and Leather. From the German of DR. EMIL WINCKLER and LOUIS E. ANDES. The whole translated and edited by WILLIAM T. BRANNT. With 11 illustrations. 12mo. $2.50

ARLOT.—A Complete Guide for Coach Painters:

Translated from the French of M. ARLOT, Coach Painter; for eleven years Foreman of Painting to M. Eherler, Coach Maker, Paris. By A. A. FESQUET, Chemist and Engineer. To which is added an Appendix, containing Information respecting the Materials and the Practice of Coach and Car Painting and Varnishing in the United States and Great Britain. 12mo. . . . $1.25

Heat Produced per Bell

C in Fuel = a }
C in CO^2 of Charge = b } = Total C in Gas

C to CO = (a − b) × 2400

C of this CO to CO^2 = C in CO^2 of Gas × 5600

Wgt. of Blast × Temp in Deg C × ~~.239~~ .23–

ARMENGAUD, AMOROUX, AND JOHNSON.—The Practical Draughtsman's Book of Industrial Design, and Machinist's and Engineer's Drawing Companion:

Forming a Complete Course of Mechanical Engineering and Architectural Drawing. From the French of M. Armengaud the elder, Prof. of Design in the Conservatoire of Arts and Industry, Paris, and MM. Armengaud the younger, and Amoroux, Civil Engineers. Rewritten and arranged with additional matter and plates, selections from and examples of the most useful and generally employed mechanism of the day. By WILLIAM JOHNSON, Assoc. Inst. C. E. Illustrated by fifty folio steel plates, and fifty wood-cuts. A new edition, 4to., half morocco $10.00

ARMSTRONG.—The Construction and Management of Steam Boilers:

By R. ARMSTRONG, C. E. With an Appendix by ROBERT MALLET, C. E., F. R. S. Seventh Edition. Illustrated. 1 vol. 12mo. 75

ARROWSMITH.—Paper-Hanger's Companion:

A Treatise in which the Practical Operations of the Trade are Systematically laid down: with Copious Directions Preparatory to Papering; Preventives against the Effect of Damp on Walls; the various Cements and Pastes Adapted to the Several Purposes of the Trade; Observations and Directions for the Panelling and Ornamenting of Rooms, etc. By JAMES ARROWSMITH. 12mo., cloth $1.25

ASHTON.—The Theory and Practice of the Art of Designing Fancy Cotton and Woollen Cloths from Sample:

Giving full instructions for reducing drafts, as well as the methods of spooling and making out harness for cross drafts and finding any required reed; with calculations and tables of yarn. By FREDERIC T. ASHTON, Designer, West Pittsfield, Mass. With fifty-two illustrations. One vol. folio $10.00

AUERBACH—CROOKES.—Anthracen:

Its Constitution, Properties, Manufacture and Derivatives, including Artificial Alizarin, Anthrapurpurin, etc., with their applications in Dyeing and Printing. By G. AUERBACH. Translated and edited from the revised manuscript of the Author, by WM. CROOKES, F. R. S., Vice-President of the Chemical Society. 8vo. . . $5.00

BAIRD.—Miscellaneous Papers on Economic Questions. By Henry Carey Baird. (*In preparation.*)

BAIRD.—The American Cotton Spinner, and Manager's and Carder's Guide:

A Practical Treatise on Cotton Spinning; giving the Dimensions and Speed of Machinery, Draught and Twist Calculations, etc.; with notices of recent Improvements: together with Rules and Examples for making changes in the sizes and numbers of Roving and Yarn. Compiled from the papers of the late ROBERT H. BAIRD. 12mo. $1.50

BAIRD.—Standard Wages Computing Tables:
An Improvement in all former Methods of Computation, so arranged that wages for days, hours, or fractions of hours, at a specified rate per day or hour, may be ascertained at a glance. By T. SPANGLER BAIRD. Oblong folio $5.00

BAKER.—Long-Span Railway Bridges:
Comprising Investigations of the Comparative Theoretical and Practical Advantages of the various Adopted or Proposed Type Systems of Construction; with numerous Formulæ and Tables. By B. BAKER. 12mo, ... $1.50

BAKER.—The Mathematical Theory of the Steam-Engine:
With Rules at length, and Examples worked out for the use of Practical Men. By T. BAKER, C. E., with numerous Diagrams. Sixth Edition, Revised by Prof. J. R. YOUNG. 12mo. . 75

BARLOW.—The History and Principles of Weaving, by Hand and by Power:
Reprinted, with Considerable Additions, from "Engineering," with a chapter on Lace-making Machinery, reprinted from the Journal of the "Society of Arts." By ALFRED BARLOW. With several hundred illustrations. 8vo., 443 pages $10.00

BARR.—A Practical Treatise on the Combustion of Coal:
Including descriptions of various mechanical devices for the Economic Generation of Heat by the Combustion of Fuel, whether solid, liquid or gaseous. 8vo. $2.50

BARR.—A Practical Treatise on High Pressure Steam Boilers:
Including Results of Recent Experimental Tests of Boiler Materials, together with a Description of Approved Safety Apparatus, Steam Pumps, Injectors and Economizers in actual use. By WM. M. BARR. 204 Illustrations. 8vo. $3.00

BAUERMAN.—A Treatise on the Metallurgy of Iron:
Containing Outlines of the History of Iron Manufacture, Methods of Assay, and Analysis of Iron Ores, Processes of Manufacture of Iron and Steel, etc., etc. By H. BAUERMAN, F. G. S., Associate of the Royal School of Mines. Fifth Edition, Revised and Enlarged. Illustrated with numerous Wood Engravings from Drawings by J. B. JORDAN. 12mo. $2.00

BAYLES.—House Drainage and Water Service:
In Cities, Villages and Rural Neighborhoods. With Incidental Consideration of Certain Causes Affecting the Healthfulness of Dwellings. By JAMES C. BAYLES, Editor of "The Iron Age" and "The Metal Worker." With numerous illustrations. 8vo. cloth, $3.00

BEANS.—A Treatise on Railway Curves and Location of Railroads:
By E. W. BEANS, C. E. Illustrated. 12mo. Tucks . $1.50

BECKETT.—A Rudimentary Treatise on Clocks, and Watches and Bells:
By Sir EDMUND BECKETT, Bart., LL. D., Q. C. F. R. A. S. With numerous illustrations. Seventh Edition, Revised and Enlarged. 12mo. $2.25

BELL.—Carpentry Made Easy:
Or, The Science and Art of Framing on a New and Improved System. With Specific Instructions for Building Balloon Frames, Barn Frames, Mill Frames, Warehouses, Church Spires, etc. Comprising also a System of Bridge Building, with Bills, Estimates of Cost, and valuable Tables. Illustrated by forty-four plates, comprising nearly 200 figures. By WILLIAM E. BELL, Architect and Practical Builder. 8vo. $5.00

BEMROSE.—Fret-Cutting and Perforated Carving:
With fifty-three practical illustrations. By W. BEMROSE, JR. 1 vol. quarto $3.00

BEMROSE.—Manual of Buhl-work and Marquetry:
With Practical Instructions for Learners, and ninety colored designs. By W. BEMROSE, JR. 1 vol. quarto $3.00

BEMROSE.—Manual of Wood Carving:
With Practical Illustrations for Learners of the Art, and Original and Selected Designs. By WILLIAM BEMROSE, JR. With an Introduction by LLEWELLYN JEWITT, F. S. A., etc. With 128 illustrations, 4to. $3.00

BILLINGS.—Tobacco:
Its History, Variety, Culture, Manufacture, Commerce, and Various Modes of Use. By E. R. BILLINGS. Illustrated by nearly 200 engravings. 8vo. $3.00

BIRD.—The American Practical Dyers' Companion:
Comprising a Description of the Principal Dye-Stuffs and Chemicals used in Dyeing, their Natures and Uses; Mordants, and How Made; with the best American, English, French and German processes for Bleaching and Dyeing Silk, Wool, Cotton, Linen, Flannel, Felt, Dress Goods, Mixed and Hosiery Yarns, Feathers, Grass, Felt, Fur, Wool, and Straw Hats, Jute Yarn, Vegetable Ivory, Mats, Skins, Furs, Leather, etc., etc. By Wood, Aniline, and other Processes, together with Remarks on Finishing Agents, and Instructions in the Finishing of Fabrics, Substitutes for Indigo, Water-Proofing of Materials, Tests and Purification of Water, Manufacture of Aniline and other New Dye Wares, Harmonizing Colors, etc., etc.; embracing in all over 800 Receipts for Colors and Shades, *accompanied by* 170 *Dyed Samples of Raw Materials and Fabrics.* By F. J. BIRD, Practical Dyer, Author of "The Dyers' Hand-Book." 8vo. $10.00

BLINN.—A Practical Workshop Companion for Tin, Sheet-Iron, and Copper-plate Workers:
Containing Rules for describing various kinds of Patterns used by Tin, Sheet-Iron and Copper-plate Workers; Practical Geometry; Mensuration of Surfaces and Solids; Tables of the Weights of Metals, Lead-pipe, etc.; Tables of Areas and Circumferences of Circles; Japan, Varnishes, Lackers, Cements, Compositions, etc., etc. By LEROY J. BLINN, Master Mechanic. With over One Hundred Illustrations. 12mo. $2.50

BOOTH.—Marble Worker's Manual:
Containing Practical Information respecting Marbles in general, their Cutting, Working and Polishing; Veneering of Marble; Mosaics; Composition and Use of Artificial Marble, Stuccos, Cements, Receipts, Secrets, etc., etc. Translated from the French by M. L. BOOTH. With an Appendix concerning American Marbles. 12mo., cloth $1.50

BOOTH and MORFIT.—The Encyclopædia of Chemistry, Practical and Theoretical:
Embracing its application to the Arts, Metallurgy, Mineralogy, Geology, Medicine and Pharmacy. By JAMES C. BOOTH, Melter and Refiner in the United States Mint, Professor of Applied Chemistry in the Franklin Institute, etc., assisted by CAMPBELL MORFIT, author of "Chemical Manipulations," etc. Seventh Edition. Complete in one volume, royal 8vo., 978 pages, with numerous wood-cuts and other illustrations $5.00

BRAMWELL.—The Wool Carder's Vade-Mecum:
A Complete Manual of the Art of Carding Textile Fabrics. By W. C. BRAMWELL. Third Edition, revised and enlarged. Illustrated. Pp. 400. 12mo. $2.50

BRANNT.—A Practical Treatise on Animal and Vegetable Fats and Oils:
Comprising both Fixed and Volatile Oils, their Physical and Chemical Properties and Uses, the Manner of Extracting and Refining them, and Practical Rules for Testing them; as well as the Manufacture of Artificial Butter, Lubricants, including Mineral Lubricating Oils, etc., and on Ozokerite. Edited chiefly from the German of DRS. KARL SCHAEDLER, G. W. ASKINSON, and RICHARD BRUNNER, with Additions and Lists of American Patents relating to the Extraction, Rendering, Refining, Decomposing, and Bleaching of Fats and Oils. By WILLIAM T. BRANNT. Illustrated by 244 engravings. 739 pages. 8vo. $7.50

BRANNT.—A Practical Treatise on the Manufacture of Soap and Candles:
Based upon the most Recent Experiences in the Practice and Science; comprising the Chemistry, Raw Materials, Machinery, and Utensils and Various Processes of Manufacture, including a great variety of formulas. Edited chiefly from the German of Dr. C. Deite, A. Engelhardt, Dr. C. Schaedler and others; with additions and lists of American Patents relating to these subjects. By WM. T. BRANNT. Illustrated by 163 engravings. 677 pages. 8vo. . . . $7.50

BRANNT.—A Practical Treatise on the Raw Materials and the Distillation and Rectification of Alcohol, and the Preparation of Alcoholic Liquors, Liqueurs, Cordials, Bitters, etc.:
Edited chiefly from the German of Dr. K. Stammer, Dr. F. Elsner, and E. Schubert. By WM. T. BRANNT. Illustrated by thirty-one engravings. 12mo. $2.50

BRANNT—WAHL.—The Techno-Chemical Receipt Book:
Containing several thousand Receipts covering the latest, most important, and most useful discoveries in Chemical Technology, and their Practical Application in the Arts and the Industries. Edited chiefly from the German of Drs. Winckler, Elsner, Heintze, Mierzinski, Jacobsen, Koller, and Heinzerling, with additions by WM. T. BRANNT and WM. H. WAHL, PH. D. Illustrated by 78 engravings. 12mo. 495 pages $2.00

BROWN.—Five Hundred and Seven Mechanical Movements.
Embracing all those which are most important in Dynamics, Hydraulics, Hydrostatics, Pneumatics, Steam-Engines, Mill and other Gearing, Presses, Horology and Miscellaneous Machinery; and including many movements never before published, and several of which have only recently come into use. By HENRY T. BROWN. 12mo. $1.00

BUCKMASTER.—The Elements of Mechanical Physics:
By J. C. BUCKMASTER. Illustrated with numerous engravings. 12mo. $1.50

BULLOCK.—The American Cottage Builder:
A Series of Designs, Plans and Specifications, from $200 to $20,000, for Homes for the People; together with Warming, Ventilation, Drainage, Painting and Landscape Gardening. By JOHN BULLOCK, Architect and Editor of "The Rudiments of Architecture and Building," etc., etc. Illustrated by 75 engravings. 8vo. $3.50

BULLOCK.—The Rudiments of Architecture and Building:
For the use of Architects, Builders, Draughtsmen, Machinists, Engineers and Mechanics. Edited by JOHN BULLOCK, author of "The American Cottage Builder." Illustrated by 250 Engravings. 8vo. $3.50

BURGH.—Practical Rules for the Proportions of Modern Engines and Boilers for Land and Marine Purposes.
By N. P. BURGH, Engineer. 12mo. $1.50

BYLES.—Sophisms of Free Trade and Popular Political Economy Examined.
By a BARRISTER (SIR JOHN BARNARD BYLES, Judge of Common Pleas). From the Ninth English Edition, as published by the Manchester Reciprocity Association. 12mo. $1.25

BOWMAN.—The Structure of the Wool Fibre in its Relation to the Use of Wool for Technical Purposes:
Being the substance, with additions, of Five Lectures, delivered at the request of the Council, to the members of the Bradford Technical College, and the Society of Dyers and Colorists. By F. H. BOWMAN, D. Sc., F. R. S. E., F. L. S. Illustrated by 32 engravings. 8vo. $6.50

BYRNE.—Hand-Book for the Artisan, Mechanic, and Engineer:
Comprising the Grinding and Sharpening of Cutting Tools, Abrasive Processes, Lapidary Work, Gem and Glass Engraving, Varnishing and Lackering, Apparatus, Materials and Processes for Grinding and

Polishing, etc. By OLIVER BYRNE. Illustrated by 185 wood engravings. 8vo. $5.00

BYRNE.—Pocket-Book for Railroad and Civil Engineers:
Containing New, Exact and Concise Methods for Laying out Railroad Curves, Switches, Frog Angles and Crossings; the Staking out of work; Levelling; the Calculation of Cuttings; Embankments; Earthwork, etc. By OLIVER BYRNE. 18mo., full bound, pocket-book form $1.75

BYRNE.—The Practical Metal-Worker's Assistant:
Comprising Metallurgic Chemistry; the Arts of Working all Metals and Alloys; Forging of Iron and Steel; Hardening and Tempering; Melting and Mixing; Casting and Founding; Works in Sheet Metal; the Processes Dependent on the Ductility of the Metals; Soldering; and the most Improved Processes and Tools employed by Metal-Workers. With the Application of the Art of Electro-Metallurgy to Manufacturing Processes; collected from Original Sources, and from the works of Holtzapffel, Bergeron, Leupold, Plumier, Napier, Scoffern, Clay, Fairbairn and others. By OLIVER BYRNE. A new, revised and improved edition, to which is added an Appendix, containing The Manufacture of Russian Sheet-Iron. By JOHN PERCY, M. D., F. R. S. The Manufacture of Malleable Iron Castings, and Improvements in Bessemer Steel. By A. A. FESQUET, Chemist and Engineer. With over Six Hundred Engravings, Illustrating every Branch of the Subject. 8vo. $7.00

BYRNE.—The Practical Model Calculator:
For the Engineer, Mechanic, Manufacturer of Engine Work, Naval Architect, Miner and Millwright. By OLIVER BYRNE. 8vo., nearly 600 pages $4.50

CABINET MAKER'S ALBUM OF FURNITURE:
Comprising a Collection of Designs for various Styles of Furniture. Illustrated by Forty-eight Large and Beautifully Engraved Plates. Oblong, 8vo. $3.50

CALLINGHAM.—Sign Writing and Glass Embossing:
A Complete Practical Illustrated Manual of the Art. By JAMES CALLINGHAM. 12mo. $1.50

CAMPIN.—A Practical Treatise on Mechanical Engineering:
Comprising Metallurgy, Moulding, Casting, Forging, Tools, Workshop Machinery, Mechanical Manipulation, Manufacture of Steam-Engines, etc. With an Appendix on the Analysis of Iron and Iron Ores. By FRANCIS CAMPIN, C. E. To which are added, Observations on the Construction of Steam Boilers, and Remarks upon Furnaces used for Smoke Prevention; with a Chapter on Explosions. By R. ARMSTRONG, C. E., and JOHN BOURNE. Rules for Calculating the Change Wheels for Screws on a Turning Lathe, and for a Wheel-cutting Machine. By J. LA NICCA. Management of Steel, Including Forging, Hardening, Tempering, Annealing, Shrinking and Expansion; and the Case-hardening of Iron. By G. EDE. 8vo. Illustrated with twenty-nine plates and 100 wood engravings $5.00

CAREY.—A Memoir of Henry C. Carey.
By DR. WM. ELDER. With a portrait. 8vo., cloth . . 75

CAREY.—The Works of Henry C. Carey:
Harmony of Interests: Agricultural, Manufacturing and Commercial. 8vo. $1.50
Manual of Social Science. Condensed from Carey's "Principles of Social Science." By KATE MCKEAN. 1 vol. 12mo. . $2.25
Miscellaneous Works. With a Portrait. 2 vols. 8vo. $6.00
Past, Present and Future. 8vo. $2.50
Principles of Social Science. 3 volumes, 8vo. . . $10.00
The Slave-Trade, Domestic and Foreign; Why it Exists, and How it may be Extinguished (1853). 8vo. $2.00
The Unity of Law: As Exhibited in the Relations of Physical, Social, Mental and Moral Science (1872). 8vo. . . . $3.50

CLARK.—Tramways, their Construction and Working:
Embracing a Comprehensive History of the System. With an exhaustive analysis of the various modes of traction, including horse-power, steam, heated water and compressed air; a description of the varieties of Rolling stock, and ample details of cost and working expenses. By D. KINNEAR CLARK. Illustrated by over 200 wood engravings, and thirteen folding plates. 2 vols. 8vo. . $12.50

COLBURN.—The Locomotive Engine:
Including a Description of its Structure, Rules for Estimating its Capabilities, and Practical Observations on its Construction and Management. By ZERAH COLBURN. Illustrated. 12mo. . $1.00

COLLENS.—The Eden of Labor; or, the Christian Utopia.
By T. WHARTON COLLENS, author of "Humanics," "The History of Charity," etc. 12mo. Paper cover, $1.00; Cloth . $1.25

COOLEY.—A Complete Practical Treatise on Perfumery:
Being a Hand-book of Perfumes, Cosmetics and other Toilet Articles. With a Comprehensive Collection of Formulæ. By ARNOLD J. COOLEY. 12mo. $1.50

COOPER.—A Treatise on the use of Belting for the Transmission of Power.
With numerous illustrations of approved and actual methods of arranging Main Driving and Quarter Twist Belts, and of Belt Fastenings. Examples and Rules in great number for exhibiting and calculating the size and driving power of Belts. Plain, Particular and Practical Directions for the Treatment, Care and Management of Belts. Descriptions of many varieties of Beltings, together with chapters on the Transmission of Power by Ropes; by Iron and Wood Frictional Gearing; on the Strength of Belting Leather; and on the Experimental Investigations of Morin, Briggs, and others. By JOHN H. COOPER, M. E. 8vo. $3.50

CRAIK.—The Practical American Millwright and Miller.
By DAVID CRAIK, Millwright. Illustrated by numerous wood engravings and two folding plates. 8vo. $5.00

CREW.—A Practical Treatise on Petroleum:
Comprising its Origin, Geology, Geographical Distribution, History, Chemistry, Mining, Technology, Uses and Transportation. Together with a Description of Gas Wells, the Application of Gas as Fuel, etc. By BENJAMIN J. CREW. With an Appendix on the Product and Exhaustion of the Oil Regions, and the Geology of Natural Gas in Pennsylvania and New York. By CHARLES A. ASHBURNER, M. S Geologist in Charge Pennsylvania Survey, Philadelphia. Illustrated by 70 engravings. 8vo. 508 pages $5.00

CROOKES.—Select Methods in Chemical Analysis (Chiefly Inorganic):
By WILLIAM CROOKES, F. R. S., V. P. C. S. 2d edition, re-written and greatly enlarged. Illustrated by 37 wood-cuts. 725 pp. 8vo. $8.00

CRISTIANI.—A Technical Treatise on Soap and Candles:
With a Glance at the Industry of Fats and Oils. By R. S. CRISTIANI, Chemist. Author of "Perfumery and Kindred Arts." Illustrated by 176 engravings. 581 pages, 8vo. . . . $7.50

CRISTIANI.—Perfumery and Kindred Arts:
A Comprehensive Treatise on Perfumery, containing a History of Perfumes from the remotest ages to the present time. A complete detailed description of the various Materials and Apparatus used in the Perfumer's Art, with thorough Practical Instruction and careful Formulæ, and advice for the fabrication of all known preparations of the day, including Essences, Tinctures, Extracts, Spirits, Waters, Vinegars, Pomades, Powders, Paints, Oils, Emulsions, Cosmetics, Infusions, Pastilles, Tooth Powders and Washes, Cachous, Hair Dyes, Sachets, Essential Oils, Flavoring Extracts, etc.; and full details for making and manipulating Fancy Toilet Soaps, Shaving Creams, etc., by new and improved methods. With an Appendix giving hints and advice for making and fermenting Domestic Wines, Cordials, Liquors, Candies, Jellies, Syrups, Colors, etc., and for Perfuming and Flavoring Segars, Snuff and Tobacco, and Miscellaneous Receipts for various useful Analogous Articles. By R. S. CRISTIANI, Consulting Chemist and Perfumer, Philadelphia. 8vo. . . $5.00

DAVIDSON.—A Practical Manual of House Painting, Graining, Marbling, and Sign-Writing:
Containing full information on the processes of House Painting in Oil and Distemper, the Formation of Letters and Practice of Sign-Writing, the Principles of Decorative Art, a Course of Elementary Drawing for House Painters, Writers, etc., and a Collection of Useful Receipts. With nine colored illustrations of Woods and Marbles, and numerous wood engravings. By ELLIS A. DAVIDSON. 12mo. $3.00

DAVIES.—A Treatise on Earthy and Other Minerals and Mining:
By D. C. DAVIES, F. G. S., Mining Engineer, etc. Illustrated by 76 Engravings. 12mo. $5.00

DAVIES.—A Treatise on Metalliferous Minerals and Mining:
By D. C. DAVIES, F. G. S., Mining Engineer, Examiner of Mines, Quarries and Collieries. Illustrated by 148 engravings of Geological Formations, Mining Operations and Machinery, drawn from the practice of all parts of the world. 2d Edition, 12mo., 450 pages $5.00

DAVIES.—A Treatise on Slate and Slate Quarrying:
Scientific, Practical and Commercial. By D. C. DAVIES, F. G. S., Mining Engineer, etc. With numerous illustrations and folding plates. 12mo. $2.00

DAVIS.—A Treatise on Steam-Boiler Incrustation and Methods for Preventing Corrosion and the Formation of Scale:
By CHARLES T. DAVIS. Illustrated by 65 engravings. 8vo. $1.50

DAVIS.—The Manufacture of Paper:
Being a Description of the various Processes for the Fabrication, Coloring and Finishing of every kind of Paper, Including the Different Raw Materials and the Methods for Determining their Values, the Tools, Machines and Practical Details connected with an intelligent and a profitable prosecution of the art, with special reference to the best American Practice. To which are added a History of Paper, complete Lists of Paper-Making Materials, List of American Machines, Tools and Processes used in treating the Raw Materials, and in Making, Coloring and Finishing Paper. By CHARLES T. DAVIS. Illustrated by 156 engravings. 608 pages, 8vo. $6.00

DAVIS.—The Manufacture of Leather:
Being a description of all of the Processes for the Tanning, Tawing, Currying, Finishing and Dyeing of every kind of Leather; including the various Raw Materials and the Methods for Determining their Values; the Tools, Machines, and all Details of Importance connected with an Intelligent and Profitable Prosecution of the Art, with Special Reference to the Best American Practice. To which are added Complete Lists of all American Patents for Materials, Processes, Tools, and Machines for Tanning, Currying, etc. By CHARLES THOMAS DAVIS. Illustrated by 302 engravings and 12 Samples of Dyed Leathers. One vol., 8vo., 824 pages $10.00

DAWIDOWSKY—BRANNT.—A Practical Treatise on the Raw Materials and Fabrication of Glue, Gelatine, Gelatine Veneers and Foils, Isinglass, Cements, Pastes, Mucilages, etc.:
Based upon Actual Experience. By F. DAWIDOWSKY, Technical Chemist. Translated from the German, with extensive additions, including a description of the most Recent American Processes, by WILLIAM T. BRANNT, Graduate of the Royal Agricultural College of Eldena, Prussia. 35 Engravings. 12mo. $2.50

DE GRAFF.—The Geometrical Stair-Builders' Guide:
Being a Plain Practical System of Hand-Railing, embracing all its necessary Details, and Geometrically Illustrated by twenty-two Steel Engravings; together with the use of the most approved principles of Practical Geometry. By SIMON DE GRAFF, Architect. 4to. $2.50

DE KONINCK—DIETZ.—A Practical Manual of Chemical Analysis and Assaying:

As applied to the Manufacture of Iron from its Ores, and to Cast Iron, Wrought Iron, and Steel, as found in Commerce. By L. L. DE KONINCK, Dr. Sc., and E. DIETZ, Engineer. Edited with Notes, by ROBERT MALLET, F. R. S., F. S. G., M. I. C. E., etc. American Edition, Edited with Notes and an Appendix on Iron Ores, by A. A. FESQUET, Chemist and Engineer. 12mo. . . . $2.50

DUNCAN.—Practical Surveyor's Guide:

Containing the necessary information to make any person of common capacity, a finished land surveyor without the aid of a teacher. By ANDREW DUNCAN. Illustrated. 12mo. . . . $1.25

DUPLAIS.—A Treatise on the Manufacture and Distillation of Alcoholic Liquors:

Comprising Accurate and Complete Details in Regard to Alcohol from Wine, Molasses, Beets, Grain, Rice, Potatoes, Sorghum, Asphodel, Fruits, etc.; with the Distillation and Rectification of Brandy, Whiskey, Rum, Gin, Swiss Absinthe, etc., the Preparation of Aromatic Waters, Volatile Oils or Essences, Sugars, Syrups, Aromatic Tinctures, Liqueurs, Cordial Wines, Effervescing Wines, etc., the Ageing of Brandy and the improvement of Spirits, with Copious Directions and Tables for Testing and Reducing Spirituous Liquors, etc., etc. Translated and Edited from the French of MM. DUPLAIS, Ainè et Jeune. By M. MCKENNIE, M. D. To which are added the United States Internal Revenue Regulations for the Assessment and Collection of Taxes on Distilled Spirits. Illustrated by fourteen folding plates and several wood engravings. 743 pp. 8vo. $10 00

DUSSAUCE.—Practical Treatise on the Fabrication of Matches, Gun Cotton, and Fulminating Powder.

By Professor H. DUSSAUCE. 12mo. $3 00

DYER AND COLOR-MAKER'S COMPANION:

Containing upwards of two hundred Receipts for making Colors, on the most approved principles, for all the various styles and fabrics now in existence; with the Scouring Process, and plain Directions for Preparing, Washing-off, and Finishing the Goods. 12mo. $1 25

EDWARDS.—A Catechism of the Marine Steam-Engine,

For the use of Engineers, Firemen, and Mechanics. A Practical Work for Practical Men. By EMORY EDWARDS, Mechanical Engineer. Illustrated by sixty-three Engravings, including examples of the most modern Engines. Third edition, thoroughly revised, with much additional matter. 12mo. 414 pages . . . $2 00

EDWARDS.—Modern American Locomotive Engines,

Their Design, Construction and Management. By EMORY EDWARDS. Illustrated 12mo. $2.00

EDWARDS.—The American Steam Engineer:

Theoretical and Practical, with examples of the latest and most approved American practice in the design and construction of Steam Engines and Boilers. For the use of engineers, machinists, boilermakers, and engineering students. By EMORY EDWARDS. Fully illustrated, 419 pages. 12mo. $2.50

EDWARDS.—Modern American Marine Engines, Boilers, and Screw Propellers,

Their Design and Construction. Showing the Present Practice of the most Eminent Engineers and Marine Engine Builders in the United States. Illustrated by 30 large and elaborate plates. 4to. $5.00

EDWARDS.—The Practical Steam Engineer's Guide

In the Design, Construction, and Management of American Stationary, Portable, and Steam Fire-Engines, Steam Pumps, Boilers, Injectors, Governors, Indicators, Pistons and Rings, Safety Valves and Steam Gauges. For the use of Engineers, Firemen, and Steam Users. By EMORY EDWARDS. Illustrated by 119 engravings. 420 pages. 12mo. $2 50

EISSLER.—The Metallurgy of Gold:

A Practical Treatise on the Metallurgical Treatment of Gold-Bearing Ores, including the Processes of Concentration and Chlorination, and the Assaying, Melting, and Refining of Gold. By M. EISSLER. With 90 Illustrations. 188 pp. 12mo. $3 00

ELDER.—Conversations on the Principal Subjects of Political Economy.

By Dr. WILLIAM ELDER. 8vo. $2 50

ELDER.—Questions of the Day,

Economic and Social. By Dr. WILLIAM ELDER. 8vo. . $3 00

ELDER.—Memoir of Henry C. Carey.

By Dr. WILLIAM ELDER. 8vo. cloth. 75

ERNI.—Mineralogy Simplified.

Easy Methods of Determining and Classifying Minerals, including Ores, by means of the Blowpipe, and by Humid Chemical Analysis, based on Professor von Kobell's Tables for the Determination of Minerals, with an Introduction to Modern Chemistry. By HENRY ERNI, A.M., M.D., Professor of Chemistry. Second Edition, rewritten, enlarged and improved. 12mo. $3.00

FAIRBAIRN.—The Principles of Mechanism and Machinery of Transmission:

Comprising the Principles of Mechanism, Wheels, and Pulleys, Strength and Proportions of Shafts, Coupling of Shafts, and Engaging and Disengaging Gear. By SIR WILLIAM FAIRBAIRN, Bart. C. E. Beautifully illustrated by over 150 wood-cuts. In one volume, 12mo $2.50

FLEMING.—Narrow Gauge Railways in America.

A Sketch of their Rise, Progress, and Success. Valuable Statistics as to Grades, Curves, Weight of Rail, Locomotives, Cars, etc. By HOWARD FLEMING. Illustrated, 8vo. $1 00

FORSYTH.—Book of Designs for Headstones, Mural, and other Monuments:

Containing 78 Designs. By JAMES FORSYTH. With an Introduction by CHARLES BOUTELL, M. A. 4 to., cloth $5 00

FRANKEL—HUTTER.—A Practical Treatise on the Manufacture of Starch, Glucose, Starch-Sugar, and Dextrine:
Based on the German of LADISLAUS VON WAGNER, Professor in the Royal Technical High School, Buda-Pest, Hungary, and other authorities. By JULIUS FRANKEL, Graduate of the Polytechnic School of Hanover. Edited by ROBERT HUTTER, Chemist, Practical Manufacturer of Starch-Sugar. Illustrated by 58 engravings, covering every branch of the subject, including examples of the most Recent and Best American Machinery. 8vo., 344 pp. . $3.50

GEE.—The Goldsmith's Handbook:
Containing full instructions for the Alloying and Working of Gold, including the Art of Alloying, Melting, Reducing, Coloring, Collecting, and Refining; the Processes of Manipulation, Recovery of Waste; Chemical and Physical Properties of Gold; with a New System of Mixing its Alloys; Solders, Enamels, and other Useful Rules and Recipes. By GEORGE E. GEE. 12mo. . . $1.75

GEE.—The Silversmith's Handbook:
Containing full instructions for the Alloying and Working of Silver, including the different modes of Refining and Melting the Metal; its Solders; the Preparation of Imitation Alloys; Methods of Manipulation; Prevention of Waste; Instructions for Improving and Finishing the Surface of the Work; together with other Useful Information and Memoranda. By GEORGE E. GEE, Jeweller. Illustrated. 12mo. $1.75

GOTHIC ALBUM FOR CABINET-MAKERS:
Designs for Gothic Furniture. Twenty-three plates. Oblong $2.00

GREENWOOD.—Steel and Iron:
Comprising the Practice and Theory of the Several Methods Pursued in their Manufacture, and of their Treatment in the Rolling-Mills, the Forge, and the Foundry. By WILLIAM HENRY GREENWOOD, F. C. S. Asso. M. I. C. E., M. I. M. E., Associate of the Royal School of Mines. With 97 Diagrams, 536 pages. 12mo. . $2.00

GREGORY.—Mathematics for Practical Men:
Adapted to the Pursuits of Surveyors, Architects, Mechanics, and Civil Engineers. By OLINTHUS GREGORY. 8vo., plates. $3.00

GRIER.—Rural Hydraulics:
A Practical Treatise on Rural Household Water Supply. Giving a full description of Springs and Wells, of Pumps and Hydraulic Ram, with Instructions in Cistern Building, Laying of Pipes, etc. By W. W. GRIER. Illustrated 8vo. 75

GRIMSHAW.—Modern Milling:
Being the substance of two addresses delivered by request, at the Franklin Institute, Philadelphia, January 19th and January 27th, 1881. By ROBERT GRIMSHAW, Ph. D. Edited from the Phonographic Reports. With 28 Illustrations. 8vo. . .

GRIMSHAW.—Saws:
The History, Development, Action, Classification, and Comparison of Saws of all kinds. *With Copious Appendices.* Giving the details

of Manufacture, Filing, Setting, Gumming, etc. Care and Use of Saws; Tables of Gauges; Capacities of Saw-Mills; List of Saw-Patents, and other valuable information. By ROBERT GRIMSHAW. Second and greatly enlarged edition, *with Supplement*, and 354 Illustrations. Quarto $4.00

GRIMSHAW.—A Supplement to Grimshaw on Saws:

Containing additional practical matter, more especially relating to the Forms of Saw-Teeth, for special material and conditions, and to the Behavior of Saws under particular conditions. 120 Illustrations. By ROBERT GRIMSHAW. Quarto . . . . . .

GRISWOLD.—Railroad Engineer's Pocket Companion for the Field:

Comprising Rules for Calculating Deflection Distances and Angles, Tangential Distances and Angles, and all Necessary Tables for Engineers; also the Art of Levelling from Preliminary Survey to the Construction of Railroads, intended Expressly for the Young Engineer, together with Numerous Valuable Rules and Examples. By W. GRISWOLD. 12mo., tucks $1.75

GRUNER.—Studies of Blast Furnace Phenomena:

By M. L. GRUNER, President of the General Council of Mines of France, and lately Professor of Metallurgy at the Ecole des Mines. Translated, with the author's sanction, with an Appendix, by L. D. B. GORDON, F. R. S. E., F. G. S. 8vo. $2.50

Hand-Book of Useful Tables for the Lumberman, Farmer and Mechanic:

Containing Accurate Tables of Logs Reduced to Inch Board Measure, Plank, Scantling and Timber Measure; Wages and Rent, by Week or Month; Capacity of Granaries, Bins and Cisterns; Land Measure, Interest Tables, with Directions for Finding the Interest on any sum at 4, 5, 6, 7 and 8 per cent., and many other Useful Tables. 32 mo., boards. 186 pages 25

HASERICK.—The Secrets of the Art of Dyeing Wool, Cotton, and Linen,

Including Bleaching and Coloring Wool and Cotton Hosiery and Random Yarns. A Treatise based on Economy and Practice. By E. C. HASERICK. *Illustrated by* 323 *Dyed Patterns of the Yarns or Fabrics.* 8vo. $12.50

HATS AND FELTING:

A Practical Treatise on their Manufacture. By a Practical Hatter. Illustrated by Drawings of Machinery, etc. 8vo. . . . $1.25

HOFFER.—A Practical Treatise on Caoutchouc and Gutta Percha,

Comprising the Properties of the Raw Materials, and the manner of Mixing and Working them; with the Fabrication of Vulcanized and Hard Rubbers, Caoutchouc and Gutta Percha Compositions, Waterproof Substances, Elastic Tissues, the Utilization of Waste, etc., etc. From the German of RAIMUND HOFFER. By W. T. BRANNT. Illustrated 12mo. $2.50

HOFMANN.—A Practical Treatise on the Manufacture of Paper in all its Branches:

By CARL HOFMANN, Late Superintendent of Paper-Mills in Germany and the United States; recently Manager of the "Public Ledger" Paper-Mills, near Elkton, Maryland. Illustrated by 110 wood engravings, and five large Folding Plates. 4to., cloth; about 400 pages $35.00

HUGHES.—American Miller and Millwright's Assistant:

By WILLIAM CARTER HUGHES. 12mo. $1.50

HULME.—Worked Examination Questions in Plane Geometrical Drawing:

For the Use of Candidates for the Royal Military Academy, Woolwich; the Royal Military College, Sandhurst; the Indian Civil Engineering College, Cooper's Hill; Indian Public Works and Telegraph Departments; Royal Marine Light Infantry; the Oxford and Cambridge Local Examinations, etc. By F. EDWARD HULME, F. L. S., F. S. A., Art-Master Marlborough College. Illustrated by 300 examples. Small quarto $2.50

JERVIS.—Railroad Property:

A Treatise on the Construction and Management of Railways; designed to afford useful knowledge, in the popular style, to the holders of this class of property; as well as Railway Managers, Officers, and Agents. By JOHN B. JERVIS, late Civil Engineer of the Hudson River Railroad, Croton Aqueduct, etc. 12mo., cloth $2.00

KEENE.—A Hand-Book of Practical Gauging:

For the Use of Beginners, to which is added a Chapter on Distillation, describing the process in operation at the Custom-House for ascertaining the Strength of Wines. By JAMES B. KEENE, of H. M. Customs. 8vo. $1.25

KELLEY.—Speeches, Addresses, and Letters on Industrial and Financial Questions:

By HON. WILLIAM D. KELLEY, M. C. 544 pages, 8vo. . $3.00

KELLOGG.—A New Monetary System:

The only means of Securing the respective Rights of Labor and Property, and of Protecting the Public from Financial Revulsions. By EDWARD KELLOGG. Revised from his work on "Labor and other Capital." With numerous additions from his manuscript. Edited by MARY KELLOGG PUTNAM. Fifth edition. To which is added a Biographical Sketch of the Author. One volume, 12mo.

Paper cover $1.00

Bound in cloth 1.50

KEMLO.—Watch-Repairer's Hand-Book:

Being a Complete Guide to the Young Beginner, in Taking Apart, Putting Together, and Thoroughly Cleaning the English Lever and other Foreign Watches, and all American Watches. By F. KEMLO, Practical Watchmaker. With Illustrations. 12mo. . $1.25

KENTISH.—A Treatise on a Box of Instruments,
And the Slide Rule; with the Theory of Trigonometry and Logarithms, including Practical Geometry, Surveying, Measuring of Timber, Cask and Malt Gauging, Heights, and Distances. By THOMAS KENTISH. In one volume. 12mo. $1.25

KERL.—The Assayer's Manual:
An Abridged Treatise on the Docimastic Examination of Ores, and Furnace and other Artificial Products. By BRUNO KERL, Professor in the Royal School of Mines. Translated from the German by WILLIAM T. BRANNT. Second American edition, edited with Extensive Additions by F. LYNWOOD GARRISON, Member of the American Institute of Mining Engineers, etc. Illustrated by 87 engravings. 8vo. $3.00

KICK.—Flour Manufacture.
A Treatise on Milling Science and Practice. By FREDERICK KICK, Imperial Regierungsrath, Professor of Mechanical Technology in the Imperial German Polytechnic Institute, Prague. Translated from the second enlarged and revised edition with supplement by H. H. P. POWLES, Assoc. Memb. Institution of Civil Engineers. Illustrated with 28 Plates, and 167 Wood-cuts. 367 pages. 8vo. . $10.00

KINGZETT.—The History, Products, and Processes of the Alkali Trade:
Including the most Recent Improvements. By CHARLES THOMAS KINGZETT, Consulting Chemist. With 23 illustrations. 8vo. $2.50

KINSLEY.—Self-Instructor on Lumber Surveying:
For the Use of Lumber Manufacturers, Surveyors, and Teachers. By CHARLES KINSLEY, Practical Surveyor and Teacher of Surveying. 12mo. $2.00

KIRK.—The Founding of Metals:
A Practical Treatise on the Melting of Iron, with a Description of the Founding of Alloys; also, of all the Metals and Mineral Substances used in the Art of Founding. Collected from original sources. By EDWARD KIRK, Practical Foundryman and Chemist. Illustrated. Third edition. 8vo. $2.50

LANDRIN.—A Treatise on Steel:
Comprising its Theory, Metallurgy, Properties, Practical Working, and Use. By M. H. C. LANDRIN, JR., Civil Engineer. Translated from the French, with Notes, by A. A. FESQUET, Chemist and Engineer. With an Appendix on the Bessemer and the Martin Processes for Manufacturing Steel, from the Report of Abram S. Hewitt United States Commissioner to the Universal Exposition, Paris, 1867. 12mo. $3.00

LARDEN.—A School Course on Heat:
By W. LARDEN, M. A. 321 pp. 12mo. $2.00

LARDNER.—The Steam-Engine:
For the Use of Beginners. By DR. LARDNER. Illustrated. 12mo. 75

LARKIN.—The Practical Brass and Iron Founder's Guide:
A Concise Treatise on Brass Founding, Moulding, the Metals and their Alloys, etc.; to which are added Recent Improvements in the Manufacture of Iron, Steel by the Bessemer Process, etc., etc. By JAMES LARKIN, late Conductor of the Brass Foundry Department in Reany, Neafie & Co.'s Penn Works, Philadelphia. Fifth edition, revised, with extensive additions. 12mo. $2.25

LEROUX.—A Practical Treatise on the Manufacture of Worsteds and Carded Yarns:
Comprising Practical Mechanics, with Rules and Calculations applied to Spinning; Sorting, Cleaning, and Scouring Wools; the English and French Methods of Combing, Drawing, and Spinning Worsteds, and Manufacturing Carded Yarns. Translated from the French of CHARLES LEROUX, Mechanical Engineer and Superintendent of a Spinning-Mill, by HORATIO PAINE, M. D., and A. A. FESQUET, Chemist and Engineer. Illustrated by twelve large Plates. To which is added an Appendix, containing Extracts from the Reports of the International Jury, and of the Artisans selected by the Committee appointed by the Council of the Society of Arts, London, on Woolen and Worsted Machinery and Fabrics, as exhibited in the Paris Universal Exposition, 1867. 8vo. $5.00

LEFFEL.—The Construction of Mill-Dams:
Comprising also the Building of Race and Reservoir Embankments and Head-Gates, the Measurement of Streams, Gauging of Water Supply, etc. By JAMES LEFFEL & Co. Illustrated by 58 engravings. 8vo. $2.50

LESLIE.—Complete Cookery:
Directions for Cookery in its Various Branches. By MISS LESLIE. Sixtieth thousand. Thoroughly revised, with the addition of New Receipts. In 12mo., cloth $1.50

LIEBER.—Assayer's Guide:
Or, Practical Directions to Assayers, Miners, and Smelters, for the Tests and Assays, by Heat and by Wet Processes, for the Ores of all the principal Metals, of Gold and Silver Coins and Alloys, and of Coal, etc. By OSCAR M. LIEBER. 12mo. $1.25

Lockwood's Dictionary of Terms:
Used in the Practice of Mechanical Engineering, embracing those Current in the Drawing Office, Pattern Shop, Foundry, Fitting, Turning, Smith's and Boiler Shops, etc., etc., comprising upwards of Six Thousand Definitions. Edited by a Foreman Pattern Maker, author of "Pattern Making." 417 pp. 12mo. $3.00

LOVE.—The Art of Dyeing, Cleaning, Scouring, and Finishing, on the Most Approved English and French Methods:
Being Practical Instructions in Dyeing Silks, Woolens, and Cottons, Feathers, Chips, Straw, etc. Scouring and Cleaning Bed and Window Curtains, Carpets, Rugs, etc. French and English Cleaning, any Color or Fabric of Silk, Satin, or Damask. By THOMAS LOVE, a Working Dyer and Scourer. Second American Edition, to which

are added General Instructions for the use of Aniline Colors. 8vo. 343 pages . . . .

LUKIN.—Amongst Machines:

Embracing Descriptions of the various Mechanical Appliances used in the Manufacture of Wood, Metal, and other Substances. 12mo. $1.75

LUKIN.—The Boy Engineers:

What They Did, and How They Did It. With 30 plates. 18mo. $1.75

LUKIN.—The Young Mechanic:

Practical Carpentry. Containing Directions for the Use of all kinds of Tools, and for Construction of Steam-Engines and Mechanical Models, including the Art of Turning in Wood and Metal. By JOHN LUKIN, Author of "The Lathe and Its Uses," etc. Illustrated. 12mo. $1.75

MAIN and BROWN.—Questions on Subjects Connected with the Marine Steam-Engine:

And Examination Papers; with Hints for their Solution. By THOMAS J. MAIN, Professor of Mathematics, Royal Naval College, and THOMAS BROWN, Chief Engineer, R. N. 12mo., cloth . $1.50

MAIN and BROWN.—The Indicator and Dynamometer:

With their Practical Applications to the Steam-Engine. By THOMAS J. MAIN, M. A. F. R., Ass't S. Professor Royal Naval College, Portsmouth, and THOMAS BROWN, Assoc. Inst. C. E., Chief Engineer R. N., attached to the R. N. College. Illustrated. 8vo. . $1.50

MAIN and BROWN.—The Marine Steam-Engine.

By THOMAS J. MAIN, F. R. Ass't S. Mathematical Professor at the Royal Naval College, Portsmouth, and THOMAS BROWN, Assoc. Inst. C. E., Chief Engineer R. N. Attached to the Royal Naval College. With numerous illustrations. 8vo. . . . $5.00

MARTIN.—Screw-Cutting Tables, for the Use of Mechanical Engineers:

Showing the Proper Arrangement of Wheels for Cutting the Threads of Screws of any Required Pitch; with a Table for Making the Universal Gas-Pipe Thread and Taps. By W. A. MARTIN, Engineer. 8vo. 50

MICHELL.—Mine Drainage:

Being a Complete and Practical Treatise on Direct-Acting Underground Steam Pumping Machinery. With a Description of a large number of the best known Engines, their General Utility and the Special Sphere of their Action, the Mode of their Application, and their Merits compared with other Pumping Machinery. By STEPHEN MICHELL. Illustrated by 137 engravings. 8vo., 277 pages . $6.00

MOLESWORTH.—Pocket-Book of Useful Formulæ and Memoranda for Civil and Mechanical Engineers.

By GUILFORD L. MOLESWORTH, Member of the Institution of Civil Engineers, Chief Resident Engineer of the Ceylon Railway. Full-bound in Pocket-book form $1.00

MOORE.—The Universal Assistant and the Complete Mechanic:

Containing over one million Industrial Facts, Calculations, Receipts, Processes, Trades Secrets, Rules, Business Forms, Legal Items, Etc., in every occupation, from the Household to the Manufactory. By R. MOORE. Illustrated by 500 Engravings. 12mo. . $2.50

MORRIS.—Easy Rules for the Measurement of Earthworks:

By means of the Prismoidal Formula. Illustrated with Numerous Wood-Cuts, Problems, and Examples, and concluded by an Extensive Table for finding the Solidity in cubic yards from Mean Areas. The whole being adapted for convenient use by Engineers, Surveyors, Contractors, and others needing Correct Measurements of Earthwork. By ELWOOD MORRIS, C. E. 8vo. $1.50

MORTON.—The System of Calculating Diameter, Circumference, Area, and Squaring the Circle:

Together with Interest and Miscellaneous Tables, and other information. By JAMES MORTON. Second Edition, enlarged, with the Metric System. 12mo. $1.00

NAPIER.—Manual of Electro-Metallurgy:

Including the Application of the Art to Manufacturing Processes. By JAMES NAPIER. Fourth American, from the Fourth London edition, revised and enlarged. Illustrated by engravings. 8vo.

NAPIER.—A System of Chemistry Applied to Dyeing.

By JAMES NAPIER, F. C. S. A New and Thoroughly Revised Edition. Completely brought up to the present state of the Science, including the Chemistry of Coal Tar Colors, by A. A. FESQUET, Chemist and Engineer. With an Appendix on Dyeing and Calico Printing, as shown at the Universal Exposition, Paris, 1867. Illustrated. 8vo. 422 pages $5.00

NEVILLE.—Hydraulic Tables, Coefficients, and Formulæ, for finding the Discharge of Water from Orifices, Notches, Weirs, Pipes, and Rivers:

Third Edition, with Additions, consisting of New Formulæ for the Discharge from Tidal and Flood Sluices and Siphons; general information on Rainfall, Catchment-Basins, Drainage, Sewerage, Water Supply for Towns and Mill Power. By JOHN NEVILLE, C. E. M. R. I. A.; Fellow of the Royal Geological Society of Ireland. Thick 12mo. $5.50

NEWBERY.—Gleanings from Ornamental Art of every style:

Drawn from Examples in the British, South Kensington, Indian, Crystal Palace, and other Museums, the Exhibitions of 1851 and 1862, and the best English and Foreign works. In a series of 100 exquisitely drawn Plates, containing many hundred examples. By ROBERT NEWBERY. 4to. $12.50

NICHOLLS.—The Theoretical and Practical Boiler-Maker and Engineer's Reference Book:

Containing a variety of Useful Information for Employers of Labor. Foremen and Working Boiler-Makers, Iron, Copper, and Tinsmiths.

Draughtsmen, Engineers, the General Steam-using Public, and for the Use of Science Schools and Classes. By SAMUEL NICHOLLS. Illustrated by sixteen plates, 12mo. $2.50

NICHOLSON.—A Manual of the Art of Bookbinding:

Containing full instructions in the different Branches of Forwarding, Gilding, and Finishing. Also, the Art of Marbling Book-edges and Paper. By JAMES B. NICHOLSON. Illustrated. 12mo., cloth $2.25

NICOLLS.—The Railway Builder:

A Hand-Book for Estimating the Probable Cost of American Railway Construction and Equipment. By WILLIAM J. NICOLLS, Civil Engineer. Illustrated, full bound, pocket-book form . $2.00

NORMANDY.—The Commercial Handbook of Chemical Analysis:

Or Practical Instructions for the Determination of the Intrinsic or Commercial Value of Substances used in Manufactures, in Trades, and in the Arts. By A. NORMANDY. New Edition, Enlarged, and to a great extent rewritten. By HENRY M. NOAD, Ph.D., F.R.S., thick 12mo. $5.00

NORRIS.—A Handbook for Locomotive Engineers and Machinists:

Comprising the Proportions and Calculations for Constructing Locomotives; Manner of Setting Valves; Tables of Squares, Cubes, Areas, etc., etc. By SEPTIMUS NORRIS, M. E. New edition. Illustrated, 12mo. $1.50

NYSTROM.—A New Treatise on Elements of Mechanics:

Establishing Strict Precision in the Meaning of Dynamical Terms: accompanied with an Appendix on Duodenal Arithmetic and Metrology. By JOHN W. NYSTROM, C. E. Illustrated. 8vo. $2.00

NYSTROM.—On Technological Education and the Construction of Ships and Screw Propellers:

For Naval and Marine Engineers. By JOHN W. NYSTROM, late Acting Chief Engineer, U. S. N. Second edition, revised, with additional matter. Illustrated by seven engravings. 12mo. . $1.50

O'NEILL.—A Dictionary of Dyeing and Calico Printing:

Containing a brief account of all the Substances and Processes in use in the Art of Dyeing and Printing Textile Fabrics; with Practical Receipts and Scientific Information. By CHARLES O'NEILL, Analytical Chemist. To which is added an Essay on Coal Tar Colors and their application to Dyeing and Calico Printing. By A. A. FESQUET, Chemist and Engineer. With an appendix on Dyeing and Calico Printing, as shown at the Universal Exposition, Paris, 1867. 8vo., 491 pages $5.00

ORTON.—Underground Treasures:

How and Where to Find Them. A Key for the Ready Determination of all the Useful Minerals within the United States. By JAMES ORTON, A.M., Late Professor of Natural History in Vassar College, N. Y.; Cor. Mem. of the Academy of Natural Sciences, Philadelphia, and of the Lyceum of Natural History, New York; author of the "Andes and the Amazon," etc. A New Edition, with Additions. Illustrated $1.50

OSBORN.—The Metallurgy of Iron and Steel:
Theoretical and Practical in all its Branches; with special reference to American Materials and Processes. By H. S. OSBORN, LL. D., Professor of Mining and Metallurgy in Lafayette College, Easton, Pennsylvania. Illustrated by numerous large folding plates and wood-engravings. 8vo. $25.00

OSBORN.—A Practical Manual of Minerals, Mines and Mining:
Comprising the Physical Properties, Geologic Positions, Local Occurrence and Associations of the Useful Minerals; their Methods of Chemical Analysis and Assay: together with Various Systems of Excavating and Timbering, Brick and Masonry Work, during Driving, Lining, Bracing and other Operations, etc. By Prof. H. S. OSBORN, LL. D., Author of the "Metallurgy of Iron and Steel." Illustrated by 171 engravings from original drawings. 8vo. $4.50

OVERMAN.—The Manufacture of Steel:
Containing the Practice and Principles of Working and Making Steel. A Handbook for Blacksmiths and Workers in Steel and Iron, Wagon Makers, Die Sinkers, Cutlers, and Manufacturers of Files and Hardware, of Steel and Iron, and for Men of Science and Art. By FREDERICK OVERMAN, Mining Engineer, Author of the "Manufacture of Iron," etc. A new, enlarged, and revised Edition. By A. A. FESQUET, Chemist and Engineer. 12mo. . . $1.50

OVERMAN.—The Moulder's and Founder's Pocket Guide:
A Treatise on Moulding and Founding in Green-sand, Dry-sand, Loam, and Cement; the Moulding of Machine Frames, Mill-gear, Hollow-ware, Ornaments, Trinkets, Bells, and Statues; Description of Moulds for Iron, Bronze, Brass, and other Metals; Plaster of Paris, Sulphur, Wax, etc.; the Construction of Melting Furnaces, the Melting and Founding of Metals; the Composition of Alloys and their Nature, etc., etc. By FREDERICK OVERMAN, M. E. A new Edition, to which is added a Supplement on Statuary and Ornamental Moulding, Ordnance, Malleable Iron Castings, etc. By A. A. FESQUET, Chemist and Engineer. Illustrated by 44 engravings. 12mo. . $2.00

PAINTER, GILDER, AND VARNISHER'S COMPANION:
Containing Rules and Regulations in everything relating to the Arts of Painting, Gilding, Varnishing, Glass-Staining, Graining, Marbling, Sign-Writing, Gilding on Glass, and Coach Painting and Varnishing; Tests for the Detection of Adulterations in Oils, Colors, etc.; and a Statement of the Diseases to which Painters are peculiarly liable, with the Simplest and Best Remedies. Sixteenth Edition. Revised, with an Appendix. Containing Colors and Coloring—Theoretical and Practical. Comprising descriptions of a great variety of Additional Pigments, their Qualities and Uses, to which are added, Dryers, and Modes and Operations of Painting, etc. Together with Chevreul's Principles of Harmony and Contrast of Colors. 12mo. Cloth $1.50

PALLETT.—The Miller's, Millwright's. and Engineer's Guide.
By HENRY PALLETT. Illustrated. 12mo. . . . $2.00

PERCY.—The Manufacture of Russian Sheet-Iron.

By JOHN PERCY, M.D., F.R.S., Lecturer on Metallurgy at the Royal School of Mines, and to The Advance Class of Artillery Officers at the Royal Artillery Institution, Woolwich; Author of "Metallurgy." With Illustrations. 8vo., paper . . 50 cts.

PERKINS.—Gas and Ventilation:

Practical Treatise on Gas and Ventilation. With Special Relation to Illuminating, Heating, and Cooking by Gas. Including Scientific Helps to Engineer-students and others. With Illustrated Diagrams. By E. E. PERKINS. 12mo., cloth $1.25

PERKINS AND STOWE.—A New Guide to the Sheet-iron and Boiler Plate Roller:

Containing a Series of Tables showing the Weight of Slabs and Piles to Produce Boiler Plates, and of the Weight of Piles and the Sizes of Bars to produce Sheet-iron; the Thickness of the Bar Gauge in decimals; the Weight per foot, and the Thickness on the Bar or Wire Gauge of the fractional parts of an inch; the Weight per sheet, and the Thickness on the Wire Gauge of Sheet-iron of various dimensions to weigh 112 lbs. per bundle; and the conversion of Short Weight into Long Weight, and Long Weight into Short. Estimated and collected by G. H. PERKINS and J. G. STOWE. $2.50

POWELL—CHANCE—HARRIS.—The Principles of Glass Making.

By HARRY J. POWELL, B. A. Together with Treatises on Crown and Sheet Glass; by HENRY CHANCE, M. A. And Plate Glass, by H. G. HARRIS, Asso. M. Inst. C. E. Illustrated 18mo. . $1.50

PROCTOR.—A Pocket-Book of Useful Tables and Formulæ for Marine Engineers:

By FRANK PROCTOR. Second Edition, Revised and Enlarged. Full-bound pocket-book form $1.50

REGNAULT.—Elements of Chemistry:

By M. V. REGNAULT. Translated from the French by T. FORREST BETTON, M. D., and edited, with Notes, by JAMES C. BOOTH, Melter and Refiner U. S. Mint, and WILLIAM L. FABER, Metallurgist and Mining Engineer. Illustrated by nearly 700 wood-engravings. Comprising nearly 1,500 pages. In two volumes, 8vo., cloth . $7.50

RICHARDS.—Aluminium:

Its History, Occurrence, Properties, Metallurgy and Applications, including its Alloys. By JOSEPH W. RICHARDS, A. C., Chemist and Practical Metallurgist, Member of the Deutsche Chemische Gesellschaft. Illustrated by 16 engravings. 12 mo. 346 pages $2.50

RIFFAULT, VERGNAUD, and TOUSSAINT.—A Practical Treatise on the Manufacture of Colors for Painting:

Comprising the Origin, Definition, and Classification of Colors; the Treatment of the Raw Materials; the best Formulæ and the Newest Processes for the Preparation of every description of Pigment, and the Necessary Apparatus and Directions for its Use; Dryers; the Testing, Application, and Qualities of Paints, etc., etc. By MM. RIFFAULT, VERGNAUD, and TOUSSAINT. Revised and Edited by M.

F. MALEPEYRE. Translated from the French, by A. A. FESQUET, Chemist and Engineer. Illustrated by Eighty engravings. In one vol., 8vo., 659 pages $7.50

ROPER.—A Catechism of High-Pressure, or Non-Condensing Steam-Engines:

Including the Modelling, Constructing, and Management of Steam-Engines and Steam Boilers. With valuable illustrations. By STEPHEN ROPER, Engineer. Sixteenth edition, revised and enlarged. 18mo., tucks, gilt edge $2.00

ROPER.—Engineer's Handy-Book:

Containing a full Explanation of the Steam-Engine Indicator, and its Use and Advantages to Engineers and Steam Users. With Formulæ for Estimating the Power of all Classes of Steam-Engines; also, Facts, Figures, Questions, and Tables for Engineers who wish to qualify themselves for the United States Navy, the Revenue Service, the Mercantile Marine, or to take charge of the Better Class of Stationary Steam-Engines. Sixth edition. 16mo., 690 pages, tucks, gilt edge $3.50

ROPER.—Hand-Book of Land and Marine Engines:

Including the Modelling, Construction, Running, and Management of Land and Marine Engines and Boilers. With illustrations. By STEPHEN ROPER, Engineer. Sixth edition. 12mo., tucks, gilt edge. $3.50

ROPER.—Hand-Book of the Locomotive:

Including the Construction of Engines and Boilers, and the Construction, Management, and Running of Locomotives. By STEPHEN ROPER. Eleventh edition. 18mo., tucks, gilt edge . $2.50

ROPER.—Hand-Book of Modern Steam Fire-Engines.

With illustrations. By STEPHEN ROPER, Engineer. Fourth edition, 12mo., tucks, gilt edge $3.50

ROPER.—Questions and Answers for Engineers.

This little book contains all the Questions that Engineers will be asked when undergoing an Examination for the purpose of procuring Licenses, and they are so plain that any Engineer or Fireman of ordinary intelligence may commit them to memory in a short time. By STEPHEN ROPER, Engineer. Third edition . . . $3.00

ROPER.—Use and Abuse of the Steam Boiler.

By STEPHEN ROPER, Engineer. Eighth edition, with illustrations. 18mo., tucks, gilt edge $2.00

ROSE.—The Complete Practical Machinist:

Embracing Lathe Work, Vise Work, Drills and Drilling, Taps and Dies, Hardening and Tempering, the Making and Use of Tools, Tool Grinding, Marking out Work, etc. By JOSHUA ROSE. Illustrated by 356 engravings. Thirteenth edition, thoroughly revised and in great part rewritten. In one vol., 12mo., 439 pages $2.50

ROSE.—Mechanical Drawing Self-Taught:

Comprising Instructions in the Selection and Preparation of Drawing Instruments, Elementary Instruction in Practical Mechanical Drawing, together with Examples in Simple Geometry and Elementary Mechanism, including Screw Threads, Gear Wheels, Mechanical Motions, Engines and Boilers. By JOSHUA ROSE, M. E. Illustrated by 330 engravings. 8vo., 313 pages $4.00

ROSE.—The Slide-Valve Practically Explained:
Embracing simple and complete Practical Demonstrations of the operation of each element in a Slide-valve Movement, and illustrating the effects of Variations in their Proportions by examples carefully selected from the most recent and successful practice. By JOSHUA ROSE, M. E. Illustrated by 35 engravings . $1.00

ROSS.—The Blowpipe in Chemistry, Mineralogy and Geology:
Containing all Known Methods of Anhydrous Analysis, many Working Examples, and Instructions for Making Apparatus. By LIEUT.-COLONEL W. A. ROSS, R. A., F. G. S. With 120 Illustrations. 12mo. $2.00

SHAW.—Civil Architecture:
Being a Complete Theoretical and Practical System of Building, containing the Fundamental Principles of the Art. By EDWARD SHAW, Architect. To which is added a Treatise on Gothic Architecture, etc. By THOMAS W. SILLOWAY and GEORGE M. HARDING, Architects. The whole illustrated by 102 quarto plates finely engraved on copper. Eleventh edition. 4to. $10.00

SHUNK.—A Practical Treatise on Railway Curves and Location, for Young Engineers.
By W. F. SHUNK, C. E. 12mo. Full bound pocket-book form $2.00

SLATER.—The Manual of Colors and Dye Wares.
By J. W. SLATER. 12mo. $3.75

SLOAN.—American Houses:
A variety of Original Designs for Rural Buildings. Illustrated by 26 colored engravings, with descriptive references. By SAMUEL SLOAN, Architect. 8vo. $1.50

SLOAN.—Homestead Architecture:
Containing Forty Designs for Villas, Cottages, and Farm-houses, with Essays on Style, Construction, Landscape Gardening, Furniture, etc., etc. Illustrated by upwards of 200 engravings. By SAMUEL SLOAN, Architect. 8vo. $3.50

SLOANE.—Home Experiments in Science.
By T. O'CONOR SLOANE, E. M., A. M., Ph. D. Illustrated by 91 engravings. 12mo. $1.50

SMEATON.—Builder's Pocket-Companion:
Containing the Elements of Building, Surveying, and Architecture; with Practical Rules and Instructions connected with the subject. By A. C. SMEATON, Civil Engineer, etc. 12mo. . . $1.50

SMITH.—A Manual of Political Economy.
By E. PESHINE SMITH. A New Edition, to which is added a full Index. 12mo. $1.25

SMITH.—Parks and Pleasure-Grounds:
Or Practical Notes on Country Residences, Villas, Public Parks, and Gardens. By CHARLES H. J. SMITH, Landscape Gardener and Garden Architect, etc., etc. 12mo. $2.00

SMITH.—The Dyer's Instructor:
Comprising Practical Instructions in the Art of Dyeing Silk, Cotton, Wool, and Worsted, and Woolen Goods; containing nearly 800 Receipts. To which is added a Treatise on the Art of Padding; and the Printing of Silk Warps, Skeins, and Handkerchiefs, and the various Mordants and Colors for the different styles of such work. By DAVID SMITH, Pattern Dyer. 12mo. $3.00

SMYTH.—A Rudimentary Treatise on Coal and Coal-Mining.
By WARRINGTON W. SMYTH, M. A., F. R. G., President R. G. S. of Cornwall. Fifth edition, revised and corrected. With numerous illustrations. 12mo. $1.75

SNIVELY.—A Treatise on the Manufacture of Perfumes and Kindred Toilet Articles.
By JOHN H. SNIVELY, Phr. D., Professor of Analytical Chemistry in the Tennessee College of Pharmacy. 8vo. . . . .

SNIVELY.—Tables for Systematic Qualitative Chemical Analysis.
By JOHN H. SNIVELY, Phr. D. 8vo. $1.00

SNIVELY.—The Elements of Systematic Qualitative Chemical Analysis:
A Hand-book for Beginners. By JOHN H. SNIVELY, Phr. D. 16mo. $2.00

STEWART.—The American System:
Speeches on the Tariff Question, and on Internal Improvements, principally delivered in the House of Representatives of the United States. By ANDREW STEWART, late M. C. from Pennsylvania. With a Portrait, and a Biographical Sketch. 8vo. . . . $3.00

STOKES.—The Cabinet-Maker and Upholsterer's Companion:
Comprising the Art of Drawing, as applicable to Cabinet Work; Veneering, Inlaying, and Buhl-Work; the Art of Dyeing and Staining Wood, Ivory, Bone, Tortoise-Shell, etc. Directions for Lackering, Japanning, and Varnishing; to make French Polish, Glues, Cements, and Compositions; with numerous Receipts, useful to workmen generally. By J. STOKES. Illustrated. A New Edition, with an Appendix upon French Polishing, Staining, Imitating, Varnishing, etc., etc. 12mo. $1.25

STRENGTH AND OTHER PROPERTIES OF METALS:
Reports of Experiments on the Strength and other Properties of Metals for Cannon. With a Description of the Machines for Testing Metals, and of the Classification of Cannon in service. By Officers of the Ordnance Department, U. S. Army. By authority of the Secretary of War. Illustrated by 25 large steel plates. Quarto . $10.00

SULLIVAN.—Protection to Native Industry.
By Sir EDWARD SULLIVAN, Baronet, author of "Ten Chapters on Social Reforms." 8vo. $1.50

SYME.—Outlines of an Industrial Science.

By DAVID SYME. 12mo. $2.00

TABLES SHOWING THE WEIGHT OF ROUND, SQUARE, AND FLAT BAR IRON, STEEL, ETC.,

By Measurement. Cloth 63

TAYLOR.—Statistics of Coal:

Including Mineral Bituminous Substances employed in Arts and Manufactures; with their Geographical, Geological, and Commercial Distribution and Amount of Production and Consumption on the American Continent. With Incidental Statistics of the Iron Manufacture. By R. C. TAYLOR. Second edition, revised by S. S. HALDEMAN. Illustrated by five Maps and many wood engravings. 8vo., cloth $10.00

TEMPLETON.—The Practical Examinator on Steam and the Steam-Engine:

With Instructive References relative thereto, arranged for the Use of Engineers, Students, and others. By WILLIAM TEMPLETON, Engineer. 12mo. $1.25

THAUSING.—The Theory and Practice of the Preparation of Malt and the Fabrication of Beer:

With especial reference to the Vienna Process of Brewing. Elaborated from personal experience by JULIUS E. THAUSING, Professor at the School for Brewers, and at the Agricultural Institute, Mödling, near Vienna. Translated from the German by WILLIAM T. BRANNT. Thoroughly and elaborately edited, with much American matter, and according to the latest and most Scientific Practice, by A. SCHWARZ and DR. A. H. BAUER. Illustrated by 140 Engravings. 8vo., 815 pages $10.00

THOMAS.—The Modern Practice of Photography:

By R. W. THOMAS, F. C. S. 8vo. 75

THOMPSON.—Political Economy. With Especial Reference to the Industrial History of Nations:

By ROBERT E. THOMPSON, M. A., Professor of Social Science in the University of Pennsylvania. 12mo. $1.50

THOMSON.—Freight Charges Calculator:

By ANDREW THOMSON, Freight Agent. 24mo. . . . $1.25

TURNER'S (THE) COMPANION:

Containing Instructions in Concentric, Elliptic, and Eccentric Turning; also various Plates of Chucks, Tools, and Instruments; and Directions for using the Eccentric Cutter, Drill, Vertical Cutter, and Circular Rest; with Patterns and Instructions for working them 12mo. $1.25

TURNING: Specimens of Fancy Turning Executed on the Hand or Foot-Lathe:

With Geometric, Oval, and Eccentric Chucks, and Elliptical Cutting Frame. By an Amateur. Illustrated by 30 exquisite Photographs. 4to. $3.00

URBIN—BRULL.—A Practical Guide for Puddling Iron and Steel.

By ED. URBIN, Engineer of Arts and Manufactures. A Prize Essay, read before the Association of Engineers, Graduate of the School of Mines, of Liege, Belgium, at the Meeting of 1865–6. To which is added A COMPARISON OF THE RESISTING PROPERTIES OF IRON AND STEEL. By A. BRULL. Translated from the French by A. A. FESQUET, Chemist and Engineer. 8vo. $1.00

VAILE.—Galvanized-Iron Cornice-Worker's Manual:

Containing Instructions in Laying out the Different Mitres, and Making Patterns for all kinds of Plain and Circular Work. Also, Tables of Weights, Areas and Circumferences of Circles, and other Matter calculated to Benefit the Trade. By CHARLES A. VAILE. Illustrated by twenty-one plates. 4to. $5.00

VILLE.—On Artificial Manures:

Their Chemical Selection and Scientific Application to Agriculture. A series of Lectures given at the Experimental Farm at Vincennes, during 1867 and 1874–75. By M. GEORGES VILLE. Translated and Edited by WILLIAM CROOKES, F. R. S. Illustrated by thirty-one engravings. 8vo., 450 pages $6.00

VILLE.—The School of Chemical Manures:

Or, Elementary Principles in the Use of Fertilizing Agents. From the French of M. GEO. VILLE, by A. A. FESQUET, Chemist and Engineer. With Illustrations. 12mo. $1.25

VOGDES.—The Architect's and Builder's Pocket-Companion and Price-Book:

Consisting of a Short but Comprehensive Epitome of Decimals, Duodecimals, Geometry and Mensuration; with Tables of United States Measures, Sizes, Weights, Strengths, etc., of Iron, Wood, Stone, Brick, Cement and Concretes, Quantities of Materials in given Sizes and Dimensions of Wood, Brick and Stone; and full and complete Bills of Prices for Carpenter's Work and Painting; also, Rules for Computing and Valuing Brick and Brick Work, Stone Work, Painting, Plastering, with a Vocabulary of Technical Terms, etc. By FRANK W. VOGDES, Architect, Indianapolis, Ind. Enlarged, revised, and corrected. In one volume, 368 pages, full-bound, pocket-book form, gilt edges $2.00

Cloth 1.50

WAHL.—Galvanoplastic Manipulations:

A Practical Guide for the Gold and Silver Electroplater and the Galvanoplastic Operator. Comprising the Electro-Deposition of all Metals by means of the Battery and the Dynamo-Electric Machine, as well as the most approved Processes of Deposition by Simple Immersion, with Descriptions of Apparatus, Chemical Products employed in the Art, etc. Based largely on the "Manipulations Hydroplastiques" of ALFRED ROSELEUR. By WILLIAM H. WAHL, Ph. D. (Heid), Secretary of the Franklin Institute. Illustrated by 189 engravings. 8vo., 656 pages $7.50

WALTON.—Coal-Mining Described and Illustrated:

By THOMAS H. WALTON, Mining Engineer. Illustrated by 24 large and elaborate Plates, after Actual Workings and Apparatus. $5.00

WARE.—The Sugar Beet.

Including a History of the Beet Sugar Industry in Europe, Varieties of the Sugar Beet, Examination, Soils, Tillage, Seeds and Sowing, Yield and Cost of Cultivation, Harvesting, Transportation, Conservation, Feeding Qualities of the Beet and of the Pulp, etc. By LEWIS S. WARE, C. E., M. E. Illustrated by ninety engravings. 8vo. $4.00

WARN.—The Sheet-Metal Worker's Instructor:

For Zinc, Sheet-Iron, Copper, and Tin-Plate Workers, etc. Containing a selection of Geometrical Problems; also, Practical and Simple Rules for Describing the various Patterns required in the different branches of the above Trades. By REUBEN H. WARN, Practical Tin-Plate Worker. To which is added an Appendix, containing Instructions for Boiler-Making, Mensuration of Surfaces and Solids, Rules for Calculating the Weights of different Figures of Iron and Steel, Tables of the Weights of Iron, Steel, etc. Illustrated by thirty-two Plates and thirty-seven Wood Engravings. 8vo. . $3.00

WARNER.—New Theorems, Tables, and Diagrams, for the Computation of Earth-work:

Designed for the use of Engineers in Preliminary and Final Estimates, of Students in Engineering, and of Contractors and other non-professional Computers. In two parts, with an Appendix. Part I. A Practical Treatise; Part II. A Theoretical Treatise, and the Appendix. Containing Notes to the Rules and Examples of Part I.; Explanations of the Construction of Scales, Tables, and Diagrams, and a Treatise upon Equivalent Square Bases and Equivalent Level Heights. The whole illustrated by numerous original engravings, comprising explanatory cuts for Definitions and Problems, Stereometric Scales and Diagrams, and a series of Lithographic Drawings from Models. Showing all the Combinations of Solid Forms which occur in Railroad Excavations and Embankments. By JOHN WARNER, A. M., Mining and Mechanical Engineer. Illustrated by 14 Plates. A new, revised and improved edition. 8vo. $4.00

WATSON.—A Manual of the Hand-Lathe:

Comprising Concise Directions for Working Metals of all kinds, Ivory, Bone and Precious Woods; Dyeing, Coloring, and French Polishing; Inlaying by Veneers, and various methods practised to produce Elaborate work with Dispatch, and at Small Expense. By EGBERT P. WATSON, Author of "The Modern Practice of American Machinists and Engineers." Illustrated by 78 engravings. $1.50

WATSON.—The Modern Practice of American Machinists and Engineers:

Including the Construction, Application, and Use of Drills, Lathe Tools, Cutters for Boring Cylinders, and Hollow-work generally, with the most Economical Speed for the same; the Results verified by Actual Practice at the Lathe, the Vise, and on the Floor. Together with Workshop Management, Economy of Manufacture, the Steam Engine, Boilers, Gears, Belting, etc., etc. By EGBERT P. WATSON. Illustrated by eighty-six engravings. 12mo. $2.50

WATSON.—The Theory and Practice of the Art of Weaving by Hand and Power:

With Calculations and Tables for the Use of those connected with the Trade. By JOHN WATSON, Manufacturer and Practical Machine-Maker. Illustrated by large Drawings of the best Power Looms. 8vo. $7.50

WATT.—The Art of Soap Making:

A Practical Hand-book of the Manufacture of Hard and Soft Soaps, Toilet Soaps, etc., including many New Processes, and a Chapter on the Recovery of Glycerine from Waste Leys. By ALEXANDER WATT. Ill. 12mo. $3.00

WEATHERLY.—Treatise on the Art of Boiling Sugar, Crystallizing, Lozenge-making, Comfits, Gum Goods,

And other processes for Confectionery, etc., in which are explained, in an easy and familiar manner, the various Methods of Manufacturing every Description of Raw and Refined Sugar Goods, as sold by Confectioners and others. 12mo. $1.50

WIGHTWICK.—Hints to Young Architects:

Comprising Advice to those who, while yet at school, are destined to the Profession; to such as, having passed their pupilage, are about to travel; and to those who, having completed their education, are about to practise. Together with a Model Specification involving a great variety of instructive and suggestive matter. By GEORGE WIGHTWICK, Architect. A new edition, revised and considerably enlarged; comprising Treatises on the Principles of Construction and Design. By G. HUSKISSON GUILLAUME, Architect. Numerous Illustrations. One vol. 12mo. $2.00

WILL.—Tables of Qualitative Chemical Analysis.

With an Introductory Chapter on the Course of Analysis. By Professor HEINRICH WILL, of Giessen, Germany. Third American, from the eleventh German edition. Edited by CHARLES F. HIMES, Ph. D., Professor of Natural Science, Dickinson College, Carlisle, Pa. 8vo. $1.50

WILLIAMS.—On Heat and Steam:

Embracing New Views of Vaporization, Condensation, and Explosion. By CHARLES WYE WILLIAMS, A. I. C. E. Illustrated 8vo. $3.50

WILSON.—A Treatise on Steam Boilers:

Their Strength, Construction, and Economical Working. By ROBERT WILSON. Illustrated 12mo. $2.50

WILSON.—First Principles of Political Economy:

With Reference to Statesmanship and the Progress of Civilization. By Professor W. D. WILSON, of the Cornell University. A new and revised edition. 12mo. $1.50

WOHLER.—A Hand-Book of Mineral Analysis:

By F. WÖHLER, Professor of Chemistry in the University of Göttingen. Edited by HENRY B. NASON, Professor of Chemistry in the Renssalaer Polytechnic Institute, Troy, New York. Illustrated. 12mo. $3.00

WORSSAM.—On Mechanical Saws:

From the Transactions of the Society of Engineers, 1869. By S. W. WORSSAM, JR. Illustrated by eighteen large plates. 8vo. $2.50

RECENT ADDITIONS.

ANDERSON.—The Prospector's Hand-Book:

A Guide for the Prospector and Traveler in Search of Metal Bearing or other Valuable Minerals. By J. W. ANDERSON. 52 Illustrations. 12mo. $1.50

BEAUMONT.—Woollen and Worsted Cloth Manufacture:

Being a Practical Treatise for the use of all persons employed in the manipulation of Textile Fabrics. By ROBERT BEAUMONT, M. S. A. With over 200 illustrations, including Sketches of Machinery, Designs, Cloths, etc. 391 pp. 12mo. $2.50

BRANNT.—The Metallic Alloys:

A Practical Guide for the Manufacture of all kinds of Alloys, Amalgams and Solders used by Metal Workers, especially by Bell Founders, Bronze Workers, Tinsmiths, Gold and Silver Workers, Dentists, etc., etc., as well as their Chemical and Physical Properties. Edited chiefly from the German of A. Krupp and Andreas Wildberger, with additions by WM. T. BRANNT. Illustrated. 12mo. $2.50

CROSS.—The Cotton Yarn Spinner:

Showing how the Preparation should be arranged for Differen Counts of Yarns by a System more uniform than has hitherto been practiced; by having a Standard Schedule from which we make all our Changes. By RICHARD CROSS. 122 pp. 12mo. . 75

GRANT.—A Hand-Book on the Teeth of Gears:

Their Curves, Properties, and Practical Construction. By GEORGE B. GRANT. Illustrated. Second Edition, enlarged. 8vo. $1.00

MAKINS.—A Manual of Metallurgy:

By GEORGE HOGARTH MAKINS, M. R. C. S., S. C. S. Illustrated by 100 engravings. Second edition rewritten and much enlarged. 8vo., 592 pages $3.00

POSSELT.—Technology of Textile Design:

Being a Practical Treatise on the Construction and Application of Weaves for all Textile Fabrics, with minute reference to the latest Inventions for Weaving. Containing also an Appendix, showing the Analysis and giving the Calculations necessary for the Manufacture of the various Textile Fabrics. By E. A. POSSELT, Head Master Textile Department, Pennsylvania Museum and School of Industrial Art, Philadelphia, with over 1000 illustrations. 292 pages. 4to. $5.00

POSSELT.—The Jacquard Machine Analysed and Explained:

With an Appendix on the Preparation of Jacquard Cards, and Practical Hints to Learners of Jacquard Designing. By E. A. POSSELT. With 230 illustrations and numerous diagrams. 127 pp. 4to. $3.00

ROPER.—Instructions and Suggestions for Engineers and Firemen:

By STEPHEN ROPER, Engineer $2.00

ROPER.—The Steam Boiler: Its Care and Management:

By STEPHEN ROPER, Engineer. 12mo., tuck, gilt edges . $2.00

ROPER.—The Young Engineer's Own Book:

Containing an Explanation of the Principle and Theories on which the Steam Engine as a Prime Mover is Based. By STEPHEN ROPER, Engineer. 160 illustrations, 363 pages. 18mo., tuck . $3.00

ROSE.—Modern Steam-Engines:

An Elementary Treatise upon the Steam-Engine, written in Plain language; for Use in the Workshop as well as in the Drawing Office. Giving Full Explanations of the Construction of Modern Steam-Engines: Including Diagrams showing their Actual operation. Together with Complete but Simple Explanations of the operations of Various Kinds of Valves, Valve Motions, and Link Motions, etc., thereby Enabling the Ordinary Engineer to Clearly Understand the Principles Involved in their Construction and Use, and to Plot out their Movements upon the Drawing Board. By JOSHUA ROSE, M. E. Illustrated by 422 engravings. 4to, 320 pages . . $6.00

ROSE.—Steam Boilers:

A Practical Treatise on Boiler Construction and Examination, for the Use of Practical Boiler Makers, Boiler Users, and Inspectors; and embracing in plain figures all the calculations necessary in Designing or Classifying Steam Boilers. By JOSHUA ROSE, M. E. Illustrated by 73 engravings. 250 pages. 8vo. $2.50

SULZ.—A Treatise on Beverages:

Or the Complete Practical Bottler. Full instructions for Laboratory Work, with Original Practical Recipes for all kinds of Carbonated Drinks, Mineral Waters, Flavorings, Extracts, Syrups, etc. By CHAS. HERMAN SULZ, Technical Chemist and Practical Bottler. Illustrated by 428 Engravings. 818 pp. 8vo. . . $10.00

Davis.—A Practical Treatise on the Manufacture of Bricks, Tiles, Terra-Cotta, etc.:

Including Hand-Made, Dry Clay, Tempered Clay, Soft-Mud, and Stiff-Clay Bricks, also Front, Hand-Pressed, Steam-Pressed, Re-Pressed, Ornamentally Shaped and Enamelled Bricks, Drain Tiles, Straight and Curved Sewer and Water-Pipes, Fire-Clays, Fire-Bricks, Glass Pots, Terra-Cotta, Roofing Tiles, Flooring Tiles, Art Tiles, Mosaic Plates, and Imitation of Intarsia or Inlaid Surfaces, comprising every Important Product of Clay Employed in Architecture, Engineering, the Blast Furnace, for Retorts, etc., with a History and the Actual Processes in Handling, Disintegrating, Tempering and Moulding the Clay into the Shape, Drying Naturally and Artificially, Setting, Burning with Coal, Natural Gas and Crude Oil Fuels, Enamelling in Polychromic Colors, Composition and Application of Glazes, etc., including Full Detailed Descriptions of the Most Modern Machines, Tools, Kilns and Kiln Roofs used. By CHARLES THOMAS DAVIS. Second Edition. Thoroughly Revised. Illustrated by 217 Engravings. 501 pp. 8vo. $5 00

CONTENTS.—CHAPTER I. The History of Bricks. II. General Remarks Concerning Bricks, their Size, Strength and Other Qualities, Ornamental Bricks, Architectural Terra-Cotta, Blue Bricks, Saltpetre Exudations upon Brick-Work. III. Enamelling, Glazing and Ornamenting Bricks and Tiles, Earthenware, etc. IV. Selecting Clays for Various Kinds of Bricks—The Different Varieties of Clay—The Characteristics, Qualities and Localities—How to Color Bricks Red—Kaolin—Terra-Cotta Clays—Fire Clays—Exploring, Digging and Marketing Fire Clays—Washing Clays. V. Making and Burning a Kiln of Hand-Made Bricks. VI. Manufacture of Dry Clay Bricks. VII. The Manufacture of Tempered-Clay Bricks, Including a Description of the most Modern Machinery Employed. VIII. Kilns. IX. The Manufacture of Pressed and Ornamental Bricks. X. The Manufacture of Fire-Bricks. XI. The Manufacture of Drain Tiles. XII. The Manufacture of Sewer-Pipes. XIII. The Manufacture of Roofing Tiles. XIV. The Manufacture of Architectural Terra-Cotta. XV. Ornamental Tiles, etc. Index.

www.ingramcontent.com/pod-product-compliance
Lightning Source LLC
LaVergne TN
LVHW011204110826
845150LV00006B/1318